50 South American Flavor Recipes for Home

By: Kelly Johnson

Table of Contents

- Argentinian Empanadas
- Brazilian Feijoada
- Chilean Pastel de Choclo
- Peruvian Ceviche
- Colombian Arepas
- Uruguayan Chivito
- Venezuelan Arepas
- Ecuadorian Ceviche de Camarón
- Bolivian Salteñas
- Paraguayan Sopa Paraguaya
- Brazilian Moqueca
- Argentinian Asado
- Chilean Pebre
- Peruvian Lomo Saltado
- Colombian Bandeja Paisa
- Uruguayan Milanesa
- Venezuelan Pabellón Criollo
- Ecuadorian Llapingachos
- Bolivian Pique a lo Macho
- Paraguayan Bori Bori
- Brazilian Pão de Queijo
- Argentinian Choripán
- Chilean Empanadas de Pino
- Peruvian Aji de Gallina
- Colombian Sancocho
- Uruguayan Tortas Fritas
- Venezuelan Cachapas
- Ecuadorian Hornado
- Bolivian Silpancho
- Paraguayan Mbejú
- Brazilian Coxinhas
- Argentinian Provoleta
- Chilean Cazuela
- Peruvian Causa Limeña
- Colombian Arroz con Coco
- Uruguayan Empanadas de Carne

- Venezuelan Tequeños
- Ecuadorian Seco de Pollo
- Bolivian Sopa de Maní
- Paraguayan Kiveve
- Brazilian Feijão Tropeiro
- Argentinian Milanesa
- Chilean Curanto
- Peruvian Anticuchos
- Colombian Arepas de Queso
- Uruguayan Tarta de Espinaca
- Venezuelan Hallacas
- Ecuadorian Encebollado
- Bolivian Fricassé
- Paraguayan Pira Caldo

Argentinian Empanadas

Ingredients:

For the Dough:

- 3 cups all-purpose flour
- 1/2 cup unsalted butter (cold, cut into small pieces)
- 1 teaspoon salt
- 1 large egg
- 1/2 cup cold water (adjust as needed)

For the Filling:

- 1 lb ground beef or ground chicken
- 1 medium onion, finely chopped
- 1 bell pepper (red or green), finely chopped
- 2 cloves garlic, minced
- 1/2 cup black olives, pitted and chopped
- 1/2 cup raisins (optional)
- 1 teaspoon ground cumin
- 1 teaspoon paprika
- 1/2 teaspoon chili powder
- 1/2 teaspoon dried oregano
- Salt and black pepper to taste
- 2 hard-boiled eggs, chopped
- 1/4 cup fresh parsley, chopped
- 1/4 cup grated Parmesan cheese (optional)

For Assembly:

- 1 egg, beaten (for egg wash)

Instructions:

1. **Prepare the Dough:**
    - In a large bowl, combine the flour and salt. Cut in the cold butter using a pastry cutter or your fingers until the mixture resembles coarse crumbs.
    - Add the egg and gradually mix in the cold water until the dough comes together. You may need to adjust the amount of water slightly. Knead the dough lightly on a floured surface until smooth.
    - Wrap the dough in plastic wrap and refrigerate for at least 30 minutes.
2. **Prepare the Filling:**
    - In a large skillet, cook the ground beef (or chicken) over medium heat until browned. Drain any excess fat.

- Add the chopped onion, bell pepper, and garlic to the skillet. Cook until the vegetables are softened, about 5 minutes.
- Stir in the olives, raisins (if using), cumin, paprika, chili powder, oregano, salt, and black pepper. Cook for another 2 minutes.
- Remove from heat and let the mixture cool slightly. Stir in the chopped hard-boiled eggs, parsley, and Parmesan cheese (if using).

3. **Assemble the Empanadas:**
   - Preheat your oven to 375°F (190°C). Line a baking sheet with parchment paper.
   - On a lightly floured surface, roll out the dough to about 1/8-inch thickness. Cut out circles using a 4- to 5-inch round cutter or the rim of a glass.
   - Place a spoonful of filling in the center of each dough circle. Fold the dough in half to cover the filling and press the edges together to seal. You can crimp the edges with a fork or fold them over to create a decorative edge.
   - Place the empanadas on the prepared baking sheet. Brush the tops with the beaten egg for a golden finish.

4. **Bake:**
   - Bake the empanadas in the preheated oven for 20-25 minutes, or until they are golden brown and crisp.

5. **Serve:**
   - Allow the empanadas to cool slightly before serving. They can be enjoyed warm or at room temperature.

Storage:

- Leftover empanadas can be stored in an airtight container in the refrigerator for up to 3 days. They can also be frozen for up to 3 months. Reheat in the oven to maintain crispness.

These Argentinian Empanadas are perfect for parties, as a snack, or as a main dish. Enjoy their savory and satisfying flavor!

Brazilian Feijoada

Ingredients:

For the Feijoada:

- 1 lb black beans (soaked overnight and drained)
- 1/2 lb pork shoulder, cut into chunks
- 1/2 lb chorizo or Portuguese sausage, sliced
- 1/2 lb smoked sausage or kielbasa, sliced
- 1/2 lb bacon, chopped
- 1/2 lb ham hocks or smoked pork ribs
- 1 onion, finely chopped
- 4 cloves garlic, minced
- 2 bay leaves
- 1 teaspoon paprika
- 1 teaspoon ground cumin
- 1 teaspoon dried oregano
- 1/2 teaspoon black pepper
- Salt to taste
- 4 cups chicken or vegetable broth (more if needed)
- 2 tablespoons olive oil

For Serving:

- Cooked white rice
- Sautéed collard greens (couve)
- Orange slices
- Brazilian farofa (toasted cassava flour mixture)
- Pickled peppers or hot sauce (optional)

Instructions:

1. **Prepare Beans:**
    - If you haven't soaked the beans overnight, do so in a pot with enough water to cover them by 2 inches. Drain before using.
2. **Cook Meats:**
    - In a large pot or Dutch oven, heat the olive oil over medium heat. Add the bacon and cook until crispy. Remove with a slotted spoon and set aside.
    - In the same pot, add the pork shoulder, chorizo, smoked sausage, and ham hocks. Cook until browned on all sides. Remove the meats and set aside.
3. **Sauté Aromatics:**
    - In the same pot, add the chopped onion and garlic. Sauté until softened and fragrant, about 5 minutes.
4. **Combine Ingredients:**

- Return the cooked meats to the pot. Add the soaked and drained beans, bay leaves, paprika, cumin, oregano, black pepper, and salt. Stir to combine.

5. **Add Broth and Simmer:**
   - Pour in the chicken or vegetable broth, adding enough to cover the beans and meats by about 1 inch. Bring to a boil.
   - Reduce heat to low, cover, and simmer for about 2 to 3 hours, or until the beans are tender and the stew has thickened. Stir occasionally and add more broth if needed.

6. **Adjust Seasoning:**
   - Taste and adjust seasoning with additional salt and pepper if necessary. Remove the bay leaves.

7. **Serve:**
   - Serve the Feijoada over cooked white rice. Accompany with sautéed collard greens, orange slices, farofa, and pickled peppers or hot sauce if desired.

Tips:

- Feijoada is traditionally cooked slowly to develop deep flavors, so take your time with the simmering process.
- For a richer flavor, you can also add a few drops of liquid smoke or smoked paprika.

Storage:

- Leftovers can be stored in an airtight container in the refrigerator for up to 5 days. Feijoada often tastes even better the next day as the flavors meld. It can also be frozen for up to 3 months. Thaw and reheat before serving.

Enjoy this iconic Brazilian dish that's perfect for a hearty meal with family and friends!

Chilean Pastel de Choclo

Ingredients:

For the Filling:

- 1 lb ground beef (or a mix of beef and pork)
- 1 onion, finely chopped
- 2 cloves garlic, minced
- 1 red bell pepper, finely chopped
- 1/2 cup black olives, pitted and chopped
- 1/2 cup raisins (optional)
- 1/2 cup hard-boiled eggs, chopped
- 1 tablespoon ground cumin
- 1 teaspoon paprika
- 1/2 teaspoon dried oregano
- Salt and black pepper to taste
- 2 tablespoons olive oil

For the Corn Topping:

- 4 cups fresh or frozen corn kernels (if using frozen, thaw first)
- 1/4 cup milk
- 1/4 cup unsalted butter
- 2 tablespoons sugar
- 1/2 teaspoon salt
- 1/4 teaspoon black pepper
- 1 large egg (optional, for egg wash)

Instructions:

1. **Prepare the Filling:**
    - In a large skillet or pan, heat the olive oil over medium heat. Add the chopped onion and cook until softened, about 5 minutes.
    - Add the garlic and red bell pepper, and cook for another 2-3 minutes until fragrant.
    - Add the ground beef (and pork, if using) to the pan. Cook until browned, breaking it up with a spoon as it cooks.
    - Stir in the ground cumin, paprika, oregano, salt, and black pepper. Mix well.
    - Add the black olives, raisins (if using), and chopped hard-boiled eggs. Stir to combine. Cook for another 5 minutes. Remove from heat and set aside.
2. **Prepare the Corn Topping:**
    - In a blender or food processor, combine the corn kernels, milk, butter, sugar, salt, and black pepper. Blend until smooth and creamy.

- If desired, beat the egg in a small bowl. This will be used as an egg wash to brush on top of the pie for a golden finish.
3. **Assemble the Pie:**
    - Preheat your oven to 375°F (190°C).
    - Spoon the meat mixture into a baking dish (about 9x13 inches or similar size).
    - Spread the corn topping evenly over the meat mixture, smoothing it out with a spatula. If using, brush the top with the beaten egg for a golden color.
4. **Bake:**
    - Bake in the preheated oven for 25-30 minutes, or until the corn topping is golden brown and set.
5. **Serve:**
    - Allow the Pastel de Choclo to cool for a few minutes before serving. This allows the layers to set slightly for easier serving.

Storage:

- Leftovers can be stored in an airtight container in the refrigerator for up to 4 days. It can also be frozen for up to 2 months. Reheat thoroughly before serving.

Enjoy this Chilean classic that combines savory and sweet flavors in a comforting pie!

Peruvian Ceviche

Ingredients:

- 1 lb fresh firm white fish (such as tilapia, sea bass, or snapper), skinless and boneless
- 1 cup freshly squeezed lime juice (about 8-10 limes)
- 1/2 cup freshly squeezed lemon juice (about 3-4 lemons)
- 1 small red onion, thinly sliced
- 1-2 jalapeño peppers or serrano peppers, thinly sliced (adjust to taste)
- 1/2 cup cilantro, chopped
- 1 teaspoon salt (or to taste)
- 1/2 teaspoon black pepper
- 1-2 tablespoons aji amarillo paste (optional, for authentic Peruvian flavor)
- 1/2 cup cooked corn kernels (optional, for garnish)
- 1/2 cup sliced cooked sweet potato (optional, for garnish)
- Lettuce leaves (optional, for serving)

Instructions:

1. **Prepare the Fish:**
   - Cut the fish into small, bite-sized cubes (about 1/2-inch pieces). Place the fish in a large bowl.
2. **Marinate the Fish:**
   - Pour the lime and lemon juices over the fish. The citrus juice should completely cover the fish. Add the salt and black pepper.
   - Gently toss the fish to coat it evenly in the juice. Cover and refrigerate for about 15-20 minutes, or until the fish is opaque and "cooked" by the acid. Stir occasionally to ensure even marination.
3. **Add Vegetables and Flavorings:**
   - After the fish is marinated, drain off some of the citrus juice, leaving just a small amount to mix with the other ingredients.
   - Add the thinly sliced red onion and peppers to the fish. Stir in the chopped cilantro and aji amarillo paste (if using). Adjust seasoning with additional salt and pepper to taste.
4. **Serve:**
   - If desired, garnish with cooked corn kernels and sliced sweet potato. Serve the ceviche on a bed of lettuce leaves for an extra touch.
   - Ceviche can be served immediately, or chilled until ready to serve. It is traditionally served with side dishes like Peruvian cancha (toasted corn nuts), sweet potato, or plantain chips.

Tips:

- Use the freshest fish available, as this will greatly affect the flavor and quality of the ceviche.

- The acidity from the citrus juice is what "cooks" the fish, so it's important to not over-marinate to avoid the fish becoming too mushy.
- Adjust the heat level by modifying the amount and type of peppers used.

Storage:

- Ceviche is best enjoyed fresh. It can be stored in the refrigerator for up to 1 day. The fish continues to "cook" in the citrus, so it's best eaten soon after preparation for the best texture and flavor.

Enjoy this vibrant and tangy Peruvian classic, perfect for a refreshing appetizer or light meal!

Colombian Arepas

Ingredients:

- 2 cups arepa flour (also called pre-cooked cornmeal, such as Harina PAN)
- 1 1/2 cups warm water
- 1/2 teaspoon salt
- 1 tablespoon unsalted butter or vegetable oil (optional, for added richness)
- 1 cup shredded cheese (optional, for cheese arepas; use a mild cheese like mozzarella or a Colombian cheese like queso fresco)

Instructions:

1. **Mix the Dough:**
   - In a large bowl, combine the arepa flour and salt. If using, add the shredded cheese to the dry ingredients.
   - Gradually add the warm water while stirring, until the mixture comes together. If you're adding butter or oil, incorporate it now. Mix until a soft, dough-like consistency is achieved.
2. **Knead and Rest:**
   - Knead the dough for a few minutes until smooth. Let it rest for about 5 minutes to allow the dough to hydrate fully and become easier to work with.
3. **Shape the Arepas:**
   - Divide the dough into 8-10 equal portions, depending on the size you prefer. Roll each portion into a ball, then flatten it into a round disc about 1/2 inch thick. You can use your hands or a rolling pin.
   - If the dough sticks, lightly dust your hands or the rolling surface with arepa flour.
4. **Cook the Arepas:**
   - **Grill or Pan-Fry:** Heat a skillet or griddle over medium heat. Lightly grease it with oil or butter. Place the arepas in the skillet and cook for about 5-7 minutes on each side, or until golden brown and cooked through. You should hear a sizzle and see a crisp exterior.
   - **Bake (optional):** For a softer texture, you can bake them after pan-frying. Preheat your oven to 375°F (190°C). Transfer the cooked arepas to a baking sheet and bake for 10-15 minutes to finish cooking the inside and give them a slightly crusty exterior.
5. **Serve:**
   - Serve the arepas warm. They can be enjoyed plain or with various toppings and fillings, such as cheese, ham, avocado, or any of your favorite ingredients.

Variations and Fillings:

- **Cheese Arepas:** Add shredded cheese to the dough for a cheesy flavor throughout.
- **Stuffed Arepas:** After cooking, cut them open and stuff with ingredients like grilled meats, cheese, or vegetables.

Storage:

- Arepas can be stored in an airtight container at room temperature for up to 2 days. They can also be refrigerated for up to 1 week. To reheat, you can use a skillet, toaster, or oven to crisp them up.

Enjoy these classic Colombian Arepas as a delicious and adaptable addition to your meals!

Uruguayan Chivito

Ingredients:

For the Steak:

- 1 lb beef steak (such as sirloin or ribeye), thinly sliced
- 2 tablespoons olive oil
- 2 cloves garlic, minced
- 1 teaspoon dried oregano
- Salt and black pepper to taste

For the Sandwich:

- 4 hamburger buns or sandwich rolls
- 4 slices ham
- 4 slices provolone or mozzarella cheese
- 4 large eggs (one per sandwich)
- 1 cup mayonnaise
- 2 tablespoons mustard (optional)
- 1 cup shredded lettuce
- 1 tomato, sliced
- Pickles (optional)
- 1 avocado, sliced (optional)
- Ketchup and/or hot sauce (optional)

Instructions:

1. **Prepare the Steak:**
   - In a small bowl, mix the olive oil, minced garlic, dried oregano, salt, and black pepper.
   - Rub this mixture onto both sides of the steak slices.
   - Heat a grill pan or skillet over medium-high heat. Cook the steak slices for about 2-3 minutes per side, or until cooked to your preferred level of doneness. The steak should be thin and tender.
2. **Cook the Eggs:**
   - In a separate non-stick skillet, cook the eggs to your liking (sunny-side up or fried). Season with a bit of salt and pepper.
3. **Toast the Buns:**
   - Lightly butter the hamburger buns or sandwich rolls and toast them in a skillet or oven until golden brown.
4. **Assemble the Chivito:**
   - Spread mayonnaise (and mustard, if using) on the bottom half of each bun.
   - Place a slice of ham on each bun.
   - Layer the cooked steak slices on top of the ham.

- - Add a slice of cheese over the steak and place the sandwiches under a broiler for about 1-2 minutes, or until the cheese is melted and bubbly.
  - Top with a fried egg, shredded lettuce, tomato slices, pickles, and avocado slices (if using).
  - Spread ketchup and/or hot sauce on the top bun, if desired.
5. **Serve:**
    - Place the top bun on each sandwich. Serve immediately while hot.

Tips:

- For added flavor, you can marinate the steak slices a few hours before cooking.
- The Chivito can be customized with additional toppings like sautéed mushrooms, caramelized onions, or your favorite condiments.

Storage:

- Chivitos are best enjoyed fresh, but leftover components can be stored separately in the refrigerator for up to 2 days. Reheat the steak and eggs before assembling if needed.

Enjoy this Uruguayan classic for a hearty and satisfying meal that's packed with flavor!

Venezuelan Arepas

Ingredients:

- 2 cups arepa flour (pre-cooked cornmeal, such as Harina PAN)
- 2 1/2 cups warm water
- 1 teaspoon salt
- 2 tablespoons vegetable oil or melted butter (optional, for added richness)

Instructions:

1. **Prepare the Dough:**
    - In a large bowl, combine the arepa flour and salt.
    - Gradually add the warm water, stirring continuously, until the mixture starts to come together. If using, add the vegetable oil or melted butter.
    - Mix until the dough is smooth and well combined. Let the dough rest for about 5 minutes to allow it to fully hydrate and become easier to handle.
2. **Shape the Arepas:**
    - Divide the dough into 8-10 equal portions, depending on the size you prefer. Roll each portion into a ball, then flatten it into a round disc about 1/2 inch thick. You can use your hands or a rolling pin.
    - If the dough sticks, lightly dust your hands or the rolling surface with arepa flour.
3. **Cook the Arepas:**
    - **Grill or Pan-Fry:** Heat a skillet or griddle over medium heat. Lightly grease it with oil or butter. Place the arepas in the skillet and cook for about 5-7 minutes on each side, or until golden brown and cooked through. You should hear a sizzle and see a crisp exterior.
    - **Bake (optional):** For a softer texture, you can bake them after pan-frying. Preheat your oven to 375°F (190°C). Transfer the cooked arepas to a baking sheet and bake for 10-15 minutes to finish cooking the inside and give them a slightly crusty exterior.
4. **Serve:**
    - Serve the arepas warm. They can be enjoyed plain or split open and filled with a variety of ingredients, such as cheese, ham, shredded beef, chicken, avocado, or any of your favorite fillings.

Popular Fillings:

- **Reina Pepiada:** A mixture of shredded chicken, avocado, mayonnaise, and lime juice.
- **Pabellón Criollo:** Shredded beef, black beans, and fried plantains.
- **Queso Blanco:** Fresh white cheese, like queso blanco or feta.
- **Perico:** Scrambled eggs with tomatoes and onions.

Tips:

- For a more authentic flavor, use Venezuelan arepa flour like Harina PAN, which is specifically made for arepas.
- The dough should be soft but not too sticky. Adjust the water as needed to achieve the right consistency.

Storage:

- Arepas can be stored in an airtight container at room temperature for up to 2 days. They can also be refrigerated for up to 1 week. To reheat, use a skillet or toaster to crisp them up.

Enjoy your Venezuelan Arepas with your favorite fillings for a delicious and customizable meal!

Ecuadorian Ceviche de Camarón

Ingredients:

- 1 lb large shrimp, peeled and deveined
- 1 cup freshly squeezed lime juice (about 8-10 limes)
- 1/2 cup freshly squeezed lemon juice (about 3-4 lemons)
- 1 small red onion, finely chopped
- 1-2 tomatoes, diced
- 1 cucumber, peeled, seeded, and diced
- 1-2 jalapeño peppers or serrano peppers, finely chopped (adjust to taste)
- 1/4 cup cilantro, chopped
- 2 cloves garlic, minced
- 1 teaspoon salt (or to taste)
- 1/2 teaspoon black pepper
- 1 avocado, diced (optional, for garnish)
- Cooked corn kernels or tostado (toasted corn nuts) for garnish
- Lettuce leaves or tortilla chips for serving

Instructions:

1. **Prepare the Shrimp:**
    - In a large pot, bring water to a boil. Add the shrimp and cook for 2-3 minutes, or until they turn pink and opaque. Do not overcook.
    - Remove the shrimp with a slotted spoon and immediately transfer them to a bowl of ice water to stop the cooking process. Let them cool for a few minutes, then drain and pat dry. Chop the shrimp into bite-sized pieces.
2. **Marinate the Shrimp:**
    - In a large mixing bowl, combine the chopped shrimp with the lime juice and lemon juice. Stir to coat the shrimp evenly. Let the mixture marinate in the refrigerator for about 30 minutes. This allows the citrus juices to "cook" the shrimp and infuse them with flavor.
3. **Prepare the Vegetables:**
    - While the shrimp is marinating, prepare the red onion, tomatoes, cucumber, and peppers. Add these to the bowl with the marinating shrimp.
4. **Add Seasonings and Herbs:**
    - Stir in the minced garlic, chopped cilantro, salt, and black pepper. Mix well to combine all ingredients. Adjust seasoning to taste.
5. **Serve:**
    - Garnish with diced avocado if desired. Serve the ceviche with cooked corn kernels or tostado for added texture and flavor.
    - Ceviche de Camarón can be served with lettuce leaves or tortilla chips on the side. It can also be enjoyed on its own as a refreshing and tangy appetizer.

Tips:

- For best results, use very fresh shrimp. If you are using frozen shrimp, ensure they are thoroughly thawed and patted dry before cooking.
- The acidity from the citrus juices is crucial for "cooking" the shrimp. If you prefer a stronger citrus flavor, you can adjust the amount of lime and lemon juice.

Storage:

- Ceviche is best enjoyed fresh but can be stored in an airtight container in the refrigerator for up to 1 day. The flavors continue to develop, but the shrimp can become more tender over time.

Enjoy this vibrant and flavorful Ecuadorian Ceviche de Camarón, perfect for a light and refreshing meal!

Bolivian Salteñas

Ingredients:

For the Dough:

- 4 cups all-purpose flour
- 1/2 cup unsalted butter, chilled and cubed
- 1 teaspoon salt
- 1 teaspoon sugar
- 1 large egg
- 1/2 cup cold water (more if needed)

For the Filling:

- 1 lb ground beef (or a mix of beef and pork)
- 1 tablespoon vegetable oil
- 1 medium onion, finely chopped
- 2 cloves garlic, minced
- 1 medium potato, peeled and diced
- 1/2 cup green peas (fresh or frozen)
- 1/2 cup diced carrots
- 1/2 cup olives, sliced (green or black)
- 1/2 cup raisins
- 1 tablespoon ground cumin
- 1 tablespoon paprika
- 1 teaspoon dried oregano
- 1 teaspoon chili powder (optional, for extra heat)
- Salt and black pepper to taste
- 1/4 cup chopped fresh cilantro (optional)
- 1 tablespoon all-purpose flour (for thickening)
- 1/2 cup beef or chicken broth

Instructions:

1. **Prepare the Dough:**
   - In a large bowl, mix the flour, salt, and sugar.
   - Cut in the chilled butter until the mixture resembles coarse crumbs.
   - In a separate bowl, whisk together the egg and cold water. Gradually add this to the flour mixture, stirring until a dough forms.
   - Knead the dough on a floured surface for about 5 minutes until smooth. Wrap in plastic wrap and refrigerate while you prepare the filling.
2. **Prepare the Filling:**
   - Heat the vegetable oil in a large skillet over medium heat. Add the chopped onion and cook until softened, about 5 minutes.

- Add the minced garlic and cook for another minute.
- Add the ground beef to the skillet. Cook until browned and fully cooked, breaking it up with a spoon as it cooks.
- Stir in the diced potato, carrots, green peas, olives, and raisins.
- Season with ground cumin, paprika, oregano, chili powder (if using), salt, and black pepper.
- Sprinkle the flour over the mixture and stir well. Add the broth and cook for another 5-10 minutes until the vegetables are tender and the filling is thickened.
- Stir in the chopped cilantro if using. Allow the filling to cool before assembling the salteñas.

3. **Assemble the Salteñas:**
   - Preheat your oven to 375°F (190°C).
   - On a floured surface, roll out the dough to about 1/8 inch thickness. Cut out circles using a cookie cutter or a glass (about 4-5 inches in diameter).
   - Place a generous spoonful of filling in the center of each dough circle.
   - Fold the dough over the filling to form a half-moon shape. Press the edges together to seal. You can crimp the edges with a fork or use your fingers to create a decorative seal.
   - Place the filled salteñas on a baking sheet lined with parchment paper.
4. **Bake:**
   - Bake in the preheated oven for 20-25 minutes, or until the dough is golden brown and cooked through.
5. **Serve:**
   - Let the salteñas cool slightly before serving. Enjoy them warm, ideally with a side of hot sauce or a fresh salad.

Tips:

- For a richer flavor, you can also use a mixture of ground beef and pork.
- Ensure the filling is well-cooked and slightly thickened to avoid soggy dough.

Storage:

- Leftover salteñas can be stored in an airtight container in the refrigerator for up to 3 days. They can also be frozen for up to 2 months. Reheat in the oven to restore crispness.

Enjoy these delicious Bolivian Salteñas as a tasty treat for any occasion!

Paraguayan Sopa Paraguaya

Ingredients:

- 2 cups cornmeal (preferably yellow cornmeal)
- 1 cup milk
- 1 cup grated cheese (such as queso fresco, mozzarella, or a mix)
- 1/2 cup unsalted butter, melted
- 1 medium onion, finely chopped
- 2 large eggs
- 1 teaspoon baking powder
- 1 teaspoon salt
- 1/2 teaspoon black pepper
- 1/2 cup chopped fresh cilantro (optional)

Instructions:

1. **Prepare the Ingredients:**
   - Preheat your oven to 375°F (190°C).
   - In a skillet, melt 1 tablespoon of butter and sauté the chopped onion over medium heat until translucent and softened, about 5 minutes. Set aside.
2. **Mix the Batter:**
   - In a large mixing bowl, combine the cornmeal, baking powder, salt, and black pepper.
   - In another bowl, whisk together the milk, melted butter, and eggs until well combined.
   - Add the milk mixture to the cornmeal mixture and stir until combined. Fold in the grated cheese and sautéed onions. If using, mix in the chopped cilantro.
3. **Bake:**
   - Grease a baking dish or casserole dish (about 8x8 inches or similar size) with butter or non-stick spray.
   - Pour the batter into the prepared dish and smooth the top with a spatula.
   - Bake in the preheated oven for 30-40 minutes, or until the top is golden brown and a toothpick inserted into the center comes out clean.
4. **Serve:**
   - Let the Sopa Paraguaya cool for a few minutes before cutting into squares. It can be served warm or at room temperature.

Tips:

- For a more traditional flavor, use Paraguayan cheese or a local cheese that melts well.
- If you prefer a richer dish, you can add cooked bacon or ham to the batter.

Storage:

- Sopa Paraguaya can be stored in an airtight container at room temperature for up to 2 days. It can also be refrigerated for up to a week or frozen for up to 2 months. Reheat in the oven to restore texture.

Enjoy this traditional Paraguayan dish as a flavorful side or main course!

Brazilian Moqueca

Ingredients:

- 1.5 lbs (700 g) firm white fish fillets (such as cod, snapper, or tilapia), cut into chunks
- 1/2 cup lime juice
- 4 tablespoons vegetable oil
- 1 large onion, chopped
- 4 cloves garlic, minced
- 1 red bell pepper, sliced
- 1 green bell pepper, sliced
- 2 medium tomatoes, chopped
- 1 cup coconut milk
- 1/2 cup fish stock or water
- 2 tablespoons palm oil (optional, for authentic flavor)
- 1 teaspoon ground cumin
- 1 teaspoon paprika
- 1 teaspoon cayenne pepper (optional, for heat)
- Salt and black pepper to taste
- 1/4 cup chopped fresh cilantro
- 1/4 cup chopped fresh parsley
- 1 tablespoon tomato paste (optional, for deeper flavor)
- 1-2 tablespoons sugar (optional, to balance acidity)
- Cooked white rice, for serving

Instructions:

1. **Marinate the Fish:**
   - In a bowl, toss the fish chunks with lime juice, salt, and black pepper. Let marinate for about 20-30 minutes in the refrigerator.
2. **Cook the Vegetables:**
   - Heat the vegetable oil in a large pot or Dutch oven over medium heat. Add the chopped onion and cook until softened and translucent, about 5 minutes.
   - Add the minced garlic and cook for another minute until fragrant.
   - Stir in the sliced bell peppers and cook until they start to soften, about 5 minutes.
3. **Add Tomatoes and Spices:**
   - Add the chopped tomatoes, coconut milk, and fish stock (or water) to the pot. Stir in the ground cumin, paprika, cayenne pepper (if using), and tomato paste (if using). Bring to a simmer.
4. **Simmer the Stew:**
   - Reduce the heat to low and let the mixture simmer for about 10 minutes to allow the flavors to meld together.
5. **Add the Fish:**
   - Gently add the marinated fish chunks to the pot. If using palm oil, add it now. Simmer the stew for another 10-15 minutes, or until the fish is cooked through

and flakes easily with a fork. Adjust seasoning with salt and black pepper to taste.
  - If the stew is too acidic, you can balance it with 1-2 tablespoons of sugar, if desired.
6. **Finish and Serve:**
   - Stir in the chopped cilantro and parsley just before serving.
   - Serve the moqueca hot over cooked white rice.

Tips:

- For an authentic flavor, use palm oil (dendê oil), which adds a unique color and taste. It can be found in Latin American or African grocery stores.
- Moqueca can be made with other seafood, like shrimp or a mix of fish and seafood, if you prefer.

Storage:

- Leftover moqueca can be stored in an airtight container in the refrigerator for up to 3 days. It can also be frozen for up to 2 months. Reheat gently on the stove to avoid overcooking the fish.

Enjoy this rich and aromatic Brazilian Moqueca, perfect for a comforting and flavorful meal!

Argentinian Asado

Ingredients:

- 2 cups cornmeal (preferably yellow cornmeal)
- 1 cup milk
- 1 cup grated cheese (such as queso fresco, mozzarella, or a mix)
- 1/2 cup unsalted butter, melted
- 1 medium onion, finely chopped
- 2 large eggs
- 1 teaspoon baking powder
- 1 teaspoon salt
- 1/2 teaspoon black pepper
- 1/2 cup chopped fresh cilantro (optional)

Instructions:

1. **Prepare the Ingredients:**
    - Preheat your oven to 375°F (190°C).
    - In a skillet, melt 1 tablespoon of butter and sauté the chopped onion over medium heat until translucent and softened, about 5 minutes. Set aside.
2. **Mix the Batter:**
    - In a large mixing bowl, combine the cornmeal, baking powder, salt, and black pepper.
    - In another bowl, whisk together the milk, melted butter, and eggs until well combined.
    - Add the milk mixture to the cornmeal mixture and stir until combined. Fold in the grated cheese and sautéed onions. If using, mix in the chopped cilantro.
3. **Bake:**
    - Grease a baking dish or casserole dish (about 8x8 inches or similar size) with butter or non-stick spray.
    - Pour the batter into the prepared dish and smooth the top with a spatula.
    - Bake in the preheated oven for 30-40 minutes, or until the top is golden brown and a toothpick inserted into the center comes out clean.
4. **Serve:**
    - Let the Sopa Paraguaya cool for a few minutes before cutting into squares. It can be served warm or at room temperature.

Tips:

- For a more traditional flavor, use Paraguayan cheese or a local cheese that melts well.
- If you prefer a richer dish, you can add cooked bacon or ham to the batter.

Storage:

- Sopa Paraguaya can be stored in an airtight container at room temperature for up to 2 days. It can also be refrigerated for up to a week or frozen for up to 2 months. Reheat in the oven to restore texture.

Enjoy this traditional Paraguayan dish as a flavorful side or main course!

Brazilian Moqueca
Ingredients:

- 1.5 lbs (700 g) firm white fish fillets (such as cod, snapper, or tilapia), cut into chunks
- 1/2 cup lime juice
- 4 tablespoons vegetable oil
- 1 large onion, chopped
- 4 cloves garlic, minced
- 1 red bell pepper, sliced
- 1 green bell pepper, sliced
- 2 medium tomatoes, chopped
- 1 cup coconut milk
- 1/2 cup fish stock or water
- 2 tablespoons palm oil (optional, for authentic flavor)
- 1 teaspoon ground cumin
- 1 teaspoon paprika
- 1 teaspoon cayenne pepper (optional, for heat)
- Salt and black pepper to taste
- 1/4 cup chopped fresh cilantro
- 1/4 cup chopped fresh parsley
- 1 tablespoon tomato paste (optional, for deeper flavor)
- 1-2 tablespoons sugar (optional, to balance acidity)
- Cooked white rice, for serving

Instructions:

1. **Marinate the Fish:**
    - In a bowl, toss the fish chunks with lime juice, salt, and black pepper. Let marinate for about 20-30 minutes in the refrigerator.
2. **Cook the Vegetables:**
    - Heat the vegetable oil in a large pot or Dutch oven over medium heat. Add the chopped onion and cook until softened and translucent, about 5 minutes.
    - Add the minced garlic and cook for another minute until fragrant.
    - Stir in the sliced bell peppers and cook until they start to soften, about 5 minutes.
3. **Add Tomatoes and Spices:**
    - Add the chopped tomatoes, coconut milk, and fish stock (or water) to the pot. Stir in the ground cumin, paprika, cayenne pepper (if using), and tomato paste (if using). Bring to a simmer.
4. **Simmer the Stew:**
    - Reduce the heat to low and let the mixture simmer for about 10 minutes to allow the flavors to meld together.
5. **Add the Fish:**
    - Gently add the marinated fish chunks to the pot. If using palm oil, add it now. Simmer the stew for another 10-15 minutes, or until the fish is cooked through

and flakes easily with a fork. Adjust seasoning with salt and black pepper to taste.
- If the stew is too acidic, you can balance it with 1-2 tablespoons of sugar, if desired.
6. **Finish and Serve:**
   - Stir in the chopped cilantro and parsley just before serving.
   - Serve the moqueca hot over cooked white rice.

Tips:

- For an authentic flavor, use palm oil (dendê oil), which adds a unique color and taste. It can be found in Latin American or African grocery stores.
- Moqueca can be made with other seafood, like shrimp or a mix of fish and seafood, if you prefer.

Storage:

- Leftover moqueca can be stored in an airtight container in the refrigerator for up to 3 days. It can also be frozen for up to 2 months. Reheat gently on the stove to avoid overcooking the fish.

Enjoy this rich and aromatic Brazilian Moqueca, perfect for a comforting and flavorful meal!

Argentinian Asado

Ingredients:

For the Beef:

- 4-5 lbs (1.8-2.3 kg) beef ribs (short ribs or spareribs), or a variety of cuts like flank steak, skirt steak, or ribeye
- Coarse sea salt or kosher salt

For the Chimichurri Sauce (optional but traditional):

- 1 cup fresh parsley, finely chopped
- 4 cloves garlic, minced
- 1/4 cup fresh oregano, finely chopped (or 1 tablespoon dried oregano)
- 1/4 cup red wine vinegar
- 1/2 cup olive oil
- 1 teaspoon red pepper flakes (adjust to taste)
- 1/2 teaspoon ground cumin
- Salt and black pepper to taste

Instructions:

1. **Prepare the Beef:**
   - If using beef ribs, remove the silver skin from the back of the ribs if it hasn't already been removed. This will help the meat cook more evenly and be more tender.
   - Generously season the beef with coarse sea salt or kosher salt. Let it sit at room temperature while you prepare the grill.
2. **Prepare the Chimichurri Sauce (if using):**
   - In a bowl, combine the parsley, garlic, oregano, red wine vinegar, olive oil, red pepper flakes, cumin, salt, and black pepper.
   - Mix well and let it sit for at least 30 minutes to allow the flavors to meld together. Chimichurri can be made ahead of time and stored in the refrigerator for up to a week.
3. **Prepare the Grill:**
   - Prepare a charcoal grill or wood fire. For an authentic asado, use hardwood or charcoal to get a hot, even heat. Let the coals burn until they are covered with white ash.
   - For a two-zone fire, place the coals on one side of the grill to create a hot direct heat zone and a cooler indirect heat zone on the other side.
4. **Grill the Beef:**
   - Place the beef ribs or other cuts on the grill over the hot side (direct heat) to sear and get a nice char. Grill for about 4-6 minutes per side, depending on the thickness of the meat and your desired level of doneness.

- Move the meat to the cooler side of the grill (indirect heat) to cook more slowly if needed. Continue grilling until the meat is cooked to your preference. For beef ribs, this may take 20-30 minutes, depending on the size and thickness.

5. **Rest the Meat:**
    - Once cooked, remove the meat from the grill and let it rest for 5-10 minutes. This allows the juices to redistribute and keeps the meat moist.
6. **Serve:**
    - Slice the beef ribs or other cuts into portions. Serve with the chimichurri sauce on the side. Accompany with traditional sides like grilled vegetables, potatoes, or a fresh salad.

Tips:

- For the best flavor, avoid using marinades or sauces that can burn. Traditional asado focuses on the natural flavor of the meat and the seasoning of salt.
- Cooking times can vary depending on the thickness of the meat and the heat of the grill. Use a meat thermometer to check for doneness if needed (medium-rare is around 135°F/57°C).

Storage:

- Leftover grilled beef can be stored in an airtight container in the refrigerator for up to 3 days. It can be reheated gently or enjoyed cold in sandwiches or salads.

Enjoy this classic Argentinian Asado, a celebration of great beef and grilling traditions!

Chilean Pebre

Ingredients:

- 1 cup fresh cilantro, finely chopped
- 1 small red onion, finely chopped
- 2 medium tomatoes, finely chopped
- 1-2 jalapeño peppers or serrano peppers, seeded and finely chopped (adjust to taste)
- 2 cloves garlic, minced
- 1/4 cup red wine vinegar
- 1/4 cup olive oil
- 1 teaspoon salt (or to taste)
- 1/2 teaspoon black pepper
- 1/2 teaspoon ground cumin (optional, for extra depth of flavor)
- 1 tablespoon lemon juice (optional, for extra tanginess)

Instructions:

1. **Prepare the Ingredients:**
   - Finely chop the cilantro, red onion, and tomatoes.
   - Seed and finely chop the jalapeño or serrano peppers according to your preferred level of spiciness.
2. **Combine Ingredients:**
   - In a medium bowl, combine the chopped cilantro, red onion, tomatoes, and peppers.
   - Add the minced garlic and stir to combine.
3. **Add Seasonings:**
   - Add the red wine vinegar, olive oil, salt, and black pepper to the bowl. If using, add the ground cumin and lemon juice.
   - Mix well to combine all the ingredients.
4. **Let It Marinate:**
   - Allow the pebre to sit for at least 30 minutes at room temperature to let the flavors meld together. The longer it sits, the more developed the flavors will be.
5. **Serve:**
   - Serve pebre as a condiment alongside grilled meats, such as beef or chicken, or with bread and cheese. It can also be used as a topping for sandwiches or tacos, or as a fresh side to enhance various dishes.

Tips:

- Adjust the heat level by adding more or less of the jalapeño or serrano peppers according to your taste.
- For a milder pebre, you can omit the peppers altogether or use fewer.

Storage:

- Pebre can be stored in an airtight container in the refrigerator for up to 5 days. It is best enjoyed fresh, but the flavors will continue to develop as it sits.

Enjoy this refreshing and vibrant Chilean Pebre as a flavorful addition to your meals!

Peruvian Lomo Saltado

Ingredients:

- **For the Marinade:**
    - 1 lb (450 g) sirloin steak or flank steak, cut into strips
    - 2 tablespoons soy sauce
    - 1 tablespoon red wine vinegar
    - 1 tablespoon vegetable oil
    - 2 cloves garlic, minced
    - 1 teaspoon ground cumin
    - 1 teaspoon paprika
    - Salt and black pepper to taste
- **For the Stir-Fry:**
    - 2 tablespoons vegetable oil
    - 1 large onion, sliced
    - 1 red bell pepper, sliced
    - 1 yellow bell pepper, sliced
    - 2 medium tomatoes, sliced
    - 1 cup French fries (pre-cooked or frozen)
    - 1/4 cup soy sauce
    - 1 tablespoon red wine vinegar
    - 1 tablespoon oyster sauce (optional)
    - 1/4 cup beef broth or water
    - 2 tablespoons chopped fresh cilantro (optional, for garnish)
    - Cooked white rice, for serving

Instructions:

1. **Marinate the Beef:**
    - In a bowl, combine the soy sauce, red wine vinegar, vegetable oil, minced garlic, ground cumin, paprika, salt, and black pepper.
    - Add the beef strips and toss to coat. Let the beef marinate for at least 30 minutes in the refrigerator.
2. **Cook the Fries (if not using pre-cooked):**
    - Prepare the French fries according to package instructions or make them from scratch. Set aside.
3. **Stir-Fry the Beef:**
    - Heat 2 tablespoons of vegetable oil in a large skillet or wok over high heat.
    - Add the marinated beef strips and stir-fry until browned and cooked to your desired level of doneness, about 3-5 minutes. Remove the beef from the skillet and set aside.
4. **Cook the Vegetables:**
    - In the same skillet, add a bit more oil if needed. Stir-fry the sliced onion and bell peppers until they start to soften, about 3-4 minutes.

- Add the sliced tomatoes and cook for another 1-2 minutes until they are slightly softened.

5. **Combine and Finish:**
   - Return the cooked beef to the skillet with the vegetables.
   - Add the soy sauce, red wine vinegar, oyster sauce (if using), and beef broth or water. Stir well to combine.
   - Add the French fries to the skillet and toss everything together gently until heated through and well combined.

6. **Serve:**
   - Serve Lomo Saltado hot over a bed of cooked white rice. Garnish with chopped fresh cilantro if desired.

Tips:

- For extra flavor, you can also add a splash of Peruvian Aji Amarillo sauce or a sprinkle of Aji Amarillo paste if available.
- If you prefer a slightly thicker sauce, you can mix a teaspoon of cornstarch with a tablespoon of water and add it to the stir-fry.

Storage:

- Leftover Lomo Saltado can be stored in an airtight container in the refrigerator for up to 3 days. Reheat gently on the stove or in the microwave.

Enjoy this classic Peruvian Lomo Saltado, a delicious blend of flavors and textures that brings a taste of Peru to your table!

Colombian Bandeja Paisa

Ingredients:

For the Beans:

- 1 cup dried red beans (or black beans), soaked overnight
- 1 onion, chopped
- 1 bell pepper, chopped
- 2 cloves garlic, minced
- 1 bay leaf
- 1 teaspoon ground cumin
- 1 teaspoon paprika
- Salt and black pepper to taste

For the Rice:

- 1 cup long-grain rice
- 2 cups water
- 1 tablespoon vegetable oil
- Salt to taste

For the Meat:

- 1 lb (450 g) ground beef
- 1 tablespoon vegetable oil
- 1 onion, finely chopped
- 2 cloves garlic, minced
- 1 teaspoon ground cumin
- 1 teaspoon paprika
- Salt and black pepper to taste

For the Chicharrón (Fried Pork Belly):

- 1 lb (450 g) pork belly, cut into pieces
- Salt to taste
- 1 tablespoon vegetable oil

For the Plantains:

- 2 ripe plantains, peeled and sliced
- Vegetable oil for frying
- Salt to taste

For the Additional Components:

- 4 eggs (fried or poached)
- 1 avocado, sliced
- 1 tomato, sliced
- 1 cup arepas (cornmeal cakes) or tortillas (optional, for serving)
- Fresh cilantro, chopped (for garnish)

Instructions:

1. **Prepare the Beans:**
   - Drain and rinse the soaked beans.
   - In a large pot, heat a bit of oil and sauté the chopped onion, bell pepper, and garlic until softened.
   - Add the beans, bay leaf, cumin, paprika, and enough water to cover the beans by about 2 inches.
   - Bring to a boil, then reduce heat to low and simmer for about 1.5-2 hours, or until beans are tender. Add salt and pepper to taste.
2. **Cook the Rice:**
   - Rinse the rice under cold water.
   - In a medium saucepan, heat the oil and add the rice. Stir to coat the rice in the oil for a minute.
   - Add water and salt, bring to a boil, then reduce heat to low and cover. Simmer for about 18-20 minutes, or until rice is cooked and water is absorbed.
3. **Prepare the Ground Beef:**
   - In a skillet, heat oil over medium heat. Add the chopped onion and garlic and sauté until softened.
   - Add the ground beef, cumin, paprika, salt, and pepper. Cook, breaking up the beef with a spoon, until browned and cooked through.
4. **Cook the Chicharrón:**
   - Season the pork belly pieces with salt.
   - Heat oil in a pan over medium heat. Fry the pork belly pieces until crispy and golden brown, about 10-15 minutes. Drain on paper towels.
5. **Fry the Plantains:**
   - Heat oil in a skillet over medium heat.
   - Fry the plantain slices until golden and crispy, about 2-3 minutes per side. Drain on paper towels and season with a little salt.
6. **Assemble the Bandeja Paisa:**
   - On a large platter, arrange a portion of rice, beans, ground beef, chicharrón, and plantains.
   - Add fried or poached eggs on top.
   - Garnish with avocado slices, tomato slices, and chopped cilantro.
   - Serve with arepas or tortillas if desired.

Tips:

- The traditional Bandeja Paisa often includes a variety of meats, so feel free to add additional items like grilled steak or sausage if desired.
- If you prefer a spicier version, you can add hot sauce or aji peppers.

Storage:

- Leftovers can be stored in an airtight container in the refrigerator for up to 3 days. Reheat gently on the stove or in the microwave.

Enjoy this delicious and authentic Colombian Bandeja Paisa, a true feast that captures the essence of Colombian cuisine!

Uruguayan Milanesa

Ingredients:

- 4 boneless beef steaks (such as sirloin or round, about 1/2 inch thick)
- 1 cup all-purpose flour
- 2 large eggs
- 1 cup breadcrumbs (preferably seasoned)
- 1/2 cup grated Parmesan cheese (optional, for added flavor)
- 2 cloves garlic, minced
- 1 tablespoon fresh parsley, chopped (or 1 teaspoon dried parsley)
- 1 teaspoon dried oregano
- 1 teaspoon ground paprika (optional, for color)
- Salt and black pepper to taste
- Vegetable oil, for frying
- Lemon wedges, for serving (optional)

Instructions:

1. **Prepare the Steaks:**
    - Place the steaks between two sheets of plastic wrap or parchment paper. Gently pound the steaks with a meat mallet or rolling pin until they are about 1/4 inch thick. Season with salt and black pepper.
2. **Set Up the Breading Station:**
    - In one shallow dish, place the flour.
    - In a second shallow dish, beat the eggs.
    - In a third shallow dish, combine the breadcrumbs, Parmesan cheese (if using), minced garlic, parsley, oregano, paprika (if using), salt, and black pepper.
3. **Bread the Steaks:**
    - Dredge each steak in the flour, shaking off excess.
    - Dip the floured steak into the beaten eggs, ensuring it is fully coated.
    - Press the steak into the breadcrumb mixture, coating it evenly and pressing the crumbs in to adhere.
4. **Fry the Milanesa:**
    - Heat a generous amount of vegetable oil in a large skillet over medium heat. The oil should be enough to cover the bottom of the skillet by about 1/4 inch.
    - Once the oil is hot, add the breaded steaks to the skillet. Fry in batches if necessary to avoid overcrowding.
    - Cook the steaks for about 3-4 minutes per side, or until golden brown and crispy. Adjust the heat as needed to prevent burning.
5. **Drain and Serve:**
    - Remove the cooked Milanesa from the skillet and drain on paper towels to remove excess oil.
    - Serve hot, garnished with lemon wedges if desired.

Serving Suggestions:

- Uruguayan Milanesa is commonly served with mashed potatoes, French fries, or a simple salad.
- It can also be used as a filling for sandwiches (Milanesa sandwiches) or served with a side of rice.

Tips:

- For extra flavor, you can add a pinch of cayenne pepper or other spices to the breadcrumb mixture.
- If you prefer a thicker coating, you can repeat the egg and breadcrumb steps for each steak.

Storage:

- Leftover Milanesa can be stored in an airtight container in the refrigerator for up to 3 days. Reheat in a skillet to retain crispiness, or in an oven.

Enjoy this delicious and crispy Uruguayan Milanesa, a true comfort food that is sure to please!

Venezuelan Pabellón Criollo

Ingredients:

For the Shredded Beef (Carne Mechada):

- 2 lbs (900 g) beef flank or brisket
- 1 onion, chopped
- 1 bell pepper, chopped
- 2 cloves garlic, minced
- 1 can (15 oz) diced tomatoes
- 1/4 cup tomato paste
- 1 tablespoon ground cumin
- 1 teaspoon paprika
- 1 teaspoon dried oregano
- 1/4 cup vegetable oil
- 2 cups beef broth
- 1 bay leaf
- Salt and black pepper to taste

For the Black Beans:

- 2 cups dried black beans (or 2 cans, drained and rinsed)
- 1 onion, chopped
- 2 cloves garlic, minced
- 1 bell pepper, chopped
- 1 tablespoon vegetable oil
- 1 teaspoon ground cumin
- 1/2 teaspoon paprika
- 1/2 teaspoon dried oregano
- 1 bay leaf
- Salt and black pepper to taste
- 2 cups water or vegetable broth

For the Rice:

- 2 cups long-grain rice
- 4 cups water
- 1 tablespoon vegetable oil
- Salt to taste

For the Fried Plantains:

- 2 ripe plantains, peeled and sliced
- Vegetable oil for frying
- Salt to taste

Instructions:

1. **Cook the Shredded Beef:**
   - In a large pot, heat the vegetable oil over medium heat. Add the chopped onion, bell pepper, and garlic. Sauté until softened, about 5 minutes.
   - Add the beef and cook until browned on all sides.
   - Stir in the diced tomatoes, tomato paste, ground cumin, paprika, oregano, salt, and black pepper. Cook for another 2 minutes.
   - Add the beef broth and bay leaf. Bring to a boil, then reduce heat to low and simmer for 2-3 hours, or until the beef is tender and easily shreds.
   - Remove the beef from the pot and shred it using two forks. Return the shredded beef to the pot and simmer until the sauce is thickened and the flavors are well combined. Adjust seasoning if necessary.
2. **Prepare the Black Beans:**
   - If using dried beans, rinse and soak them overnight. Drain and rinse again before cooking.
   - In a pot, heat the vegetable oil over medium heat. Add the chopped onion, garlic, and bell pepper. Sauté until softened.
   - Add the soaked beans, ground cumin, paprika, oregano, bay leaf, salt, and black pepper. Stir to combine.
   - Add water or vegetable broth to cover the beans by about 2 inches. Bring to a boil, then reduce heat and simmer until the beans are tender, about 1-1.5 hours. If using canned beans, just heat them with the seasonings.
3. **Cook the Rice:**
   - In a medium saucepan, heat the vegetable oil over medium heat. Add the rice and stir to coat in the oil.
   - Add water and salt, bring to a boil. Reduce heat to low, cover, and simmer for 18-20 minutes, or until rice is cooked and water is absorbed.
4. **Fry the Plantains:**
   - Heat vegetable oil in a skillet over medium heat.
   - Fry the plantain slices until golden brown and crispy, about 2-3 minutes per side. Drain on paper towels and season with a little salt.
5. **Assemble and Serve:**
   - Serve the shredded beef over a bed of rice with a side of black beans and fried plantains.
   - Garnish with fresh cilantro if desired.

Tips:

- You can use a slow cooker for the beef by combining all ingredients and cooking on low for 6-8 hours.
- For a more authentic touch, add a side of avocado or a simple salad.

Storage:

- Leftovers can be stored in airtight containers in the refrigerator for up to 3 days. The components can be frozen separately for up to 2 months. Reheat gently on the stove or in the microwave.

Enjoy this flavorful and comforting Venezuelan Pabellón Criollo, a dish that truly captures the essence of Venezuelan cuisine!

Ecuadorian Llapingachos

Ingredients:

For the Potato Patties:

- 2 lbs (900 g) potatoes (such as Russet or Yukon Gold)
- 1 cup grated cheese (such as queso fresco or mozzarella)
- 1/2 cup finely chopped onion
- 1/4 cup chopped fresh cilantro
- 1 tablespoon vegetable oil
- 1 egg
- 1/2 cup all-purpose flour
- Salt and black pepper to taste

For the Salsa:

- 2 medium tomatoes, finely chopped
- 1 small onion, finely chopped
- 1-2 jalapeño peppers, finely chopped (adjust to taste)
- 2 tablespoons fresh cilantro, chopped
- 2 tablespoons lime juice
- Salt and black pepper to taste

For Serving:

- 4 fried eggs (optional)
- Sliced avocado
- Steamed or boiled corn on the cob (optional)

Instructions:

1. **Prepare the Potatoes:**
    - Peel and cut the potatoes into chunks. Boil in salted water until tender, about 15-20 minutes.
    - Drain the potatoes and return them to the pot. Mash until smooth and let cool slightly.
2. **Make the Potato Mixture:**
    - In a large bowl, combine the mashed potatoes, grated cheese, chopped onion, cilantro, vegetable oil, and egg. Mix until well combined.
    - Gradually add the flour until the mixture is firm enough to form into patties. Season with salt and black pepper.
3. **Form and Cook the Patties:**
    - Divide the potato mixture into 8-10 portions and shape each portion into a flat, round patty, about 1/2 inch thick.

- Heat a bit of vegetable oil in a skillet over medium heat. Cook the patties in batches, about 4-5 minutes per side, or until golden brown and crispy. Drain on paper towels.
4. **Prepare the Salsa:**
   - In a bowl, combine the chopped tomatoes, onion, jalapeño peppers, cilantro, lime juice, salt, and black pepper. Mix well and let sit for 10-15 minutes to allow the flavors to meld.
5. **Serve:**
   - Serve the Llapingachos warm with the salsa on the side.
   - Garnish with fried eggs, sliced avocado, and steamed or boiled corn on the cob if desired.

Tips:

- For extra flavor, you can add some ground cumin or a pinch of paprika to the potato mixture.
- If the potato mixture is too sticky, add a bit more flour to make it easier to handle.

Storage:

- Leftover Llapingachos can be stored in an airtight container in the refrigerator for up to 3 days. Reheat in a skillet to retain crispiness.

Enjoy these delicious Ecuadorian Llapingachos as a tasty side dish or a main course!

Bolivian Pique a lo Macho

Ingredients:

For the Meat Mixture:

- 1 lb (450 g) beef sirloin or flank steak, cut into bite-sized pieces
- 2 sausages (chorizo or hot dogs), sliced
- 2 tablespoons vegetable oil
- 1 large onion, chopped
- 1 red bell pepper, chopped
- 1 green bell pepper, chopped
- 2 cloves garlic, minced
- 2 large tomatoes, chopped
- 1 tablespoon tomato paste
- 1 teaspoon ground cumin
- 1 teaspoon paprika
- 1 teaspoon dried oregano
- 1/2 teaspoon ground black pepper
- 1 cup beef broth
- Salt to taste

For the Fries:

- 4 large potatoes, peeled and cut into fries
- Vegetable oil for frying
- Salt to taste

For the Garnish:

- 2 boiled eggs, peeled and sliced
- 1/4 cup chopped fresh parsley
- 1/4 cup chopped green onions (optional)

Instructions:

1. **Prepare the Fries:**
    - Heat vegetable oil in a large skillet or deep fryer to 350°F (175°C).
    - Fry the potato slices in batches until golden and crispy, about 5-7 minutes per batch. Remove with a slotted spoon and drain on paper towels. Season with salt while still hot.
2. **Cook the Meat Mixture:**
    - Heat 2 tablespoons of vegetable oil in a large skillet or wok over medium-high heat.
    - Add the beef pieces and cook until browned on all sides. Remove the beef from the skillet and set aside.

- In the same skillet, add a bit more oil if needed. Sauté the chopped onion, red bell pepper, green bell pepper, and garlic until softened, about 5 minutes.
- Add the chopped tomatoes, tomato paste, ground cumin, paprika, oregano, black pepper, and salt. Cook for another 3-4 minutes until the tomatoes are softened.
- Return the browned beef and sausage slices to the skillet. Pour in the beef broth and stir to combine. Simmer for about 10-15 minutes until the sauce has thickened and the flavors are well combined.

3. **Assemble the Dish:**
    - On a large serving platter, arrange a bed of fries.
    - Spoon the meat mixture over the fries.
    - Garnish with sliced boiled eggs, chopped parsley, and green onions if desired.

Tips:

- For added heat, you can include some sliced jalapeños or hot sauce in the meat mixture.
- If you prefer a thicker sauce, you can mix a teaspoon of cornstarch with a tablespoon of water and add it to the skillet during the simmering process.

Storage:

- Leftover Pique a lo Macho can be stored in an airtight container in the refrigerator for up to 3 days. Reheat in a skillet to retain crispiness of the fries, or you can reheat the meat mixture separately and serve over freshly made fries.

Enjoy this robust and flavorful Bolivian Pique a lo Macho, a dish that's sure to satisfy with its rich combination of ingredients and bold flavors!

Paraguayan Bori Bori

Ingredients:

For the Stew:

- 1 whole chicken (about 3-4 lbs), cut into pieces
- 2 tablespoons vegetable oil
- 1 large onion, chopped
- 2 cloves garlic, minced
- 1 red bell pepper, chopped
- 2 large tomatoes, chopped
- 1 large carrot, sliced
- 1 cup green beans, chopped
- 1 cup corn kernels (fresh or frozen)
- 1 teaspoon ground cumin
- 1 teaspoon paprika
- 1/2 teaspoon dried oregano
- 4 cups chicken broth
- 1 bay leaf
- Salt and black pepper to taste

For the Cornmeal Dumplings (Bori Bori):

- 1 cup cornmeal
- 1/2 cup all-purpose flour
- 1/2 teaspoon baking powder
- 1/2 teaspoon salt
- 1/4 cup vegetable oil
- 1/4 cup grated Parmesan cheese (optional)
- 1/2 cup water or chicken broth

Instructions:

1. **Prepare the Stew:**
    - In a large pot, heat the vegetable oil over medium heat. Add the chopped onion and garlic, and sauté until softened and translucent, about 5 minutes.
    - Add the chopped red bell pepper and tomatoes. Cook for another 5 minutes until the tomatoes are softened.
    - Add the chicken pieces to the pot and brown on all sides.
    - Stir in the ground cumin, paprika, oregano, salt, and black pepper.
    - Pour in the chicken broth and add the bay leaf. Bring to a boil, then reduce heat and simmer for about 30 minutes, or until the chicken is cooked through and tender.

- 2. **Prepare the Dumplings (Bori Bori):**
    - Add the sliced carrots, green beans, and corn. Continue to simmer for another 10-15 minutes until the vegetables are tender.
- 2. **Prepare the Dumplings (Bori Bori):**
    - In a bowl, mix the cornmeal, flour, baking powder, salt, and Parmesan cheese (if using).
    - Stir in the vegetable oil and gradually add the water or chicken broth, mixing until a thick dough forms. The dough should be slightly sticky but manageable.
    - Using a spoon or your hands, form the dough into small balls (about 1 inch in diameter).
- 3. **Add the Dumplings to the Stew:**
    - Gently drop the dumplings into the simmering stew. Cover the pot and cook for 15-20 minutes, or until the dumplings are cooked through and have expanded.
- 4. **Serve:**
    - Remove the bay leaf from the stew.
    - Ladle the stew into bowls, making sure to include both the chicken and dumplings.
    - Garnish with fresh parsley if desired.

Tips:

- For a richer flavor, you can add a splash of white wine to the stew or some chopped fresh herbs like cilantro or parsley.
- If you prefer a thicker stew, you can mash some of the vegetables with a spoon or blend a portion of the stew.

Storage:

- Leftover Bori Bori can be stored in an airtight container in the refrigerator for up to 3 days. Reheat gently on the stove.

Enjoy this delicious and comforting Paraguayan Bori Bori, a classic dish that brings warmth and satisfaction to any meal!

Brazilian Pão de Queijo

Ingredients:

- 2 cups tapioca flour (also known as tapioca starch)
- 1 cup milk
- 1/2 cup unsalted butter
- 1 1/2 cups grated Parmesan cheese (or a mix of Parmesan and mozzarella for a milder taste)
- 1/2 teaspoon salt
- 1/4 teaspoon black pepper (optional)
- 2 large eggs

Instructions:

1. **Preheat the Oven:**
    - Preheat your oven to 375°F (190°C). Grease a mini muffin tin or line it with paper liners. You can also use a regular muffin tin if you prefer larger cheese breads.
2. **Prepare the Dough:**
    - In a medium saucepan, combine the milk and butter. Heat over medium heat until the butter is melted and the mixture is just starting to boil.
    - Remove from heat and stir in the tapioca flour until smooth. The mixture will be thick and a bit lumpy at first.
3. **Mix in the Cheese:**
    - Allow the mixture to cool for a few minutes so it's not too hot to handle.
    - Stir in the grated cheese until well combined. The mixture will be very thick.
4. **Add the Eggs:**
    - Add the eggs one at a time, stirring vigorously after each addition until the dough is smooth and glossy. The dough should be thick but still scoopable.
5. **Scoop the Dough:**
    - Use a small cookie scoop or tablespoon to portion the dough into the mini muffin tin. The dough will spread a little but not much, so try to fill the cups almost to the top.
6. **Bake:**
    - Bake in the preheated oven for 15-20 minutes, or until the Pão de Queijo are puffed and golden brown on top. They should be slightly crispy on the outside and soft and cheesy on the inside.
7. **Cool and Serve:**
    - Let the Pão de Queijo cool in the tin for a few minutes, then transfer to a wire rack to cool slightly before serving. They are best enjoyed warm but can be eaten at room temperature as well.

Tips:

- **Cheese:** You can use different types of cheese to vary the flavor. Manchego, Gouda, or cheddar can be good substitutes for Parmesan.
- **Tapioca Flour:** Make sure to use tapioca flour, not tapioca pearls. Tapioca flour is the fine powder that gives these cheese breads their distinctive chewy texture.

Storage:

- **Room Temperature:** Pão de Queijo can be stored at room temperature for up to 2 days in an airtight container.
- **Refrigeration:** They can be stored in the refrigerator for up to a week. Reheat in the oven to restore some of their crispiness.
- **Freezing:** They freeze well. Store in a freezer-safe bag or container for up to 2 months. Reheat directly from frozen in the oven at 350°F (175°C) for about 10-15 minutes.

Enjoy these delicious Brazilian cheese breads that are sure to delight with their cheesy, fluffy goodness!

Argentinian Choripán

Ingredients:

For the Chorizo:

- 4 Argentine-style chorizo sausages (or any good-quality pork sausages)
- 4 crusty bread rolls (such as baguette or ciabatta)
- Olive oil, for grilling

For the Chimichurri Sauce:

- 1 cup fresh parsley, finely chopped
- 4 cloves garlic, minced
- 2 tablespoons fresh oregano, finely chopped (or 1 tablespoon dried oregano)
- 1/2 cup red wine vinegar
- 1/2 cup extra-virgin olive oil
- 1/2 teaspoon red pepper flakes (optional, for heat)
- Salt and black pepper to taste

Instructions:

1. **Prepare the Chimichurri Sauce:**
    - In a bowl, combine the parsley, garlic, oregano, red wine vinegar, olive oil, and red pepper flakes (if using).
    - Mix well and season with salt and black pepper to taste. Let the chimichurri sit for at least 30 minutes to allow the flavors to meld. You can also prepare it a day in advance and store it in the refrigerator.
2. **Prepare the Chorizo:**
    - Preheat your grill to medium-high heat.
    - Lightly brush the sausages with olive oil to prevent sticking.
    - Grill the sausages, turning occasionally, for about 10-12 minutes, or until they are cooked through and have nice grill marks. The internal temperature should reach 160°F (71°C).
3. **Prepare the Bread Rolls:**
    - Slice the bread rolls in half lengthwise, but not all the way through, so they can open like a pocket.
    - If you like, you can toast the bread rolls on the grill for 1-2 minutes until they are crispy and slightly charred.
4. **Assemble the Choripán:**
    - Place a grilled chorizo sausage in each bread roll.
    - Spoon chimichurri sauce generously over the sausage.
5. **Serve:**
    - Serve the Choripán hot, with extra chimichurri sauce on the side if desired.

Tips:

- **Bread:** Use a sturdy bread roll that can hold up to the juices from the sausage and the chimichurri sauce. A crusty roll works best.
- **Chimichurri:** Adjust the amount of garlic, vinegar, and red pepper flakes to suit your taste preferences. Chimichurri can be quite tangy or mild depending on your preference.
- **Grilling:** If you don't have a grill, you can cook the chorizo sausages in a skillet or under a broiler.

Storage:

- **Chimichurri:** Store leftover chimichurri in an airtight container in the refrigerator for up to a week.
- **Chorizo:** Cooked sausages can be stored in the refrigerator for up to 3 days and reheated on the grill or in a skillet.

Enjoy this classic Argentinian street food that's perfect for a casual meal or a backyard barbecue!

Chilean Empanadas de Pino

Ingredients:

For the Filling:

- 1 lb (450 g) ground beef
- 1 large onion, finely chopped
- 2 cloves garlic, minced
- 1 tablespoon vegetable oil
- 1/2 cup beef broth
- 1/2 teaspoon ground cumin
- 1/2 teaspoon paprika
- 1/2 teaspoon dried oregano
- Salt and black pepper to taste
- 1/4 cup chopped fresh parsley
- 1/2 cup black olives, pitted and sliced
- 2 hard-boiled eggs, peeled and chopped

For the Dough:

- 4 cups all-purpose flour
- 1 teaspoon baking powder
- 1 teaspoon salt
- 1 cup unsalted butter, cold and cut into small cubes
- 1 large egg
- 1 cup cold water (more if needed)

For Assembly:

- 1 large egg, beaten (for egg wash)

Instructions:

1. **Prepare the Filling:**
   - In a large skillet, heat the vegetable oil over medium heat. Add the chopped onion and garlic, and sauté until the onion is translucent, about 5 minutes.
   - Add the ground beef to the skillet and cook until browned, breaking it up with a spoon as it cooks.
   - Stir in the beef broth, ground cumin, paprika, oregano, salt, and black pepper. Simmer for about 10 minutes, or until the liquid has reduced and the mixture is thick.
   - Remove from heat and stir in the chopped parsley, olives, and hard-boiled eggs. Let the filling cool.
2. **Prepare the Dough:**
   - In a large bowl, combine the flour, baking powder, and salt.

- Cut in the cold butter using a pastry cutter or your fingers until the mixture resembles coarse crumbs.
- In a small bowl, whisk together the egg and cold water. Add this mixture to the flour mixture and stir until the dough comes together. You may need to add a bit more water if the dough is too dry.
- Turn the dough out onto a floured surface and knead lightly until smooth. Divide the dough into two portions, wrap in plastic wrap, and refrigerate for at least 30 minutes.

3. **Assemble the Empanadas:**
   - Preheat your oven to 375°F (190°C). Line a baking sheet with parchment paper.
   - On a floured surface, roll out one portion of dough to about 1/8 inch (3 mm) thick. Use a round cutter (about 4-6 inches in diameter) to cut out circles of dough.
   - Place a spoonful of filling in the center of each dough circle.
   - Fold the dough over the filling to form a half-moon shape and crimp the edges with a fork or pinching the edges together with your fingers to seal.
   - Place the empanadas on the prepared baking sheet. Brush each empanada with the beaten egg for a golden finish.

4. **Bake:**
   - Bake in the preheated oven for 20-25 minutes, or until the empanadas are golden brown.

5. **Serve:**
   - Serve the empanadas warm or at room temperature. They are great on their own or with a side of pebre (Chilean salsa) or a fresh salad.

Tips:

- **Filling:** You can add a bit of sautéed mushrooms or bell peppers to the filling for extra flavor.
- **Dough:** If you find the dough too sticky, add a little more flour. If too dry, add a bit more cold water.

Storage:

- **Refrigeration:** Store leftover empanadas in an airtight container in the refrigerator for up to 3 days.
- **Freezing:** Freeze unbaked empanadas on a baking sheet until firm, then transfer to a freezer bag. Bake from frozen at 375°F (190°C) for 30-35 minutes.

Enjoy these delicious Chilean Empanadas de Pino, a true taste of Chilean comfort food!

Peruvian Aji de Gallina

Ingredients:

For the Chicken and Broth:

- 1 whole chicken (about 3-4 lbs), cut into pieces
- 1 large onion, chopped
- 2 cloves garlic, minced
- 2 bay leaves
- 1 teaspoon salt
- 1/2 teaspoon black pepper
- 1 carrot, chopped
- 1 celery stalk, chopped

For the Ají de Gallina Sauce:

- 3 tablespoons vegetable oil
- 1 large onion, finely chopped
- 2 cloves garlic, minced
- 1 cup ají amarillo paste (available at Latin markets or online; substitute with yellow bell pepper paste if needed)
- 1 cup chicken broth (from cooking the chicken)
- 1/2 cup evaporated milk or cream
- 1/4 cup grated Parmesan cheese
- 1/4 cup walnuts, finely chopped (optional, for added texture)
- Salt and black pepper to taste

For Serving:

- 4 cups cooked white rice
- 4-6 boiled potatoes, peeled and sliced
- 2 hard-boiled eggs, sliced (optional)
- Black olives for garnish (optional)
- Fresh parsley for garnish (optional)

Instructions:

1. **Cook the Chicken:**
    - In a large pot, add the chicken pieces, onion, garlic, bay leaves, salt, pepper, carrot, and celery. Cover with water and bring to a boil.
    - Reduce heat and simmer for about 30-40 minutes, or until the chicken is cooked through and tender.
    - Remove the chicken from the pot and let it cool slightly. Strain the broth and set aside.
2. **Shred the Chicken:**

- Once the chicken is cool enough to handle, shred the meat into small pieces, discarding the bones and skin.
3. **Prepare the Ají de Gallina Sauce:**
   - In a large skillet or pan, heat the vegetable oil over medium heat. Add the finely chopped onion and garlic, and sauté until softened and translucent, about 5 minutes.
   - Stir in the ají amarillo paste and cook for another 2-3 minutes.
   - Gradually add 1 cup of the chicken broth, stirring to combine. Simmer for 5 minutes.
   - Stir in the evaporated milk or cream and grated Parmesan cheese. If using walnuts, add them now. Simmer for another 5 minutes until the sauce is thickened.
   - Season with salt and black pepper to taste.
4. **Combine Chicken and Sauce:**
   - Add the shredded chicken to the sauce and stir to coat well. Simmer for another 5-10 minutes to allow the flavors to meld and the chicken to heat through.
5. **Serve:**
   - Serve the Ají de Gallina over a bed of cooked white rice. Accompany with boiled potato slices, and garnish with sliced hard-boiled eggs, black olives, and fresh parsley if desired.

Tips:

- **Ají Amarillo Paste:** If you can't find ají amarillo paste, you can use yellow bell pepper paste or a combination of yellow bell peppers and a bit of chili for heat.
- **Texture:** For a smoother sauce, you can blend the sauce ingredients before adding the chicken.

Storage:

- **Refrigeration:** Leftover Ají de Gallina can be stored in an airtight container in the refrigerator for up to 3 days.
- **Freezing:** It can be frozen for up to 2 months. Thaw in the refrigerator before reheating.

Enjoy this rich and flavorful Peruvian Ají de Gallina, a classic dish that brings a taste of Peru right to your table!

Colombian Sancocho

Ingredients:

For the Stew:

- 1 lb (450 g) chicken pieces (legs, thighs, or a whole chicken cut into parts)
- 1 lb (450 g) beef short ribs or stew meat
- 1/2 lb (225 g) pork ribs or pork shoulder, cut into chunks
- 2 tablespoons vegetable oil
- 1 large onion, chopped
- 3 cloves garlic, minced
- 1 large tomato, chopped
- 1 green bell pepper, chopped
- 2 bay leaves
- 1 teaspoon ground cumin
- 1 teaspoon paprika
- 1/2 teaspoon dried oregano
- 6 cups beef or chicken broth
- 2 large potatoes, peeled and cut into chunks
- 2 large carrots, peeled and sliced
- 1 plantain, peeled and sliced
- 1 cup yuca (cassava), peeled and cut into chunks
- 1 ear of corn, cut into 3-4 pieces
- 1/4 cup chopped fresh cilantro
- Salt and black pepper to taste

For Serving:

- 4 cups cooked white rice
- 1 avocado, sliced
- Lime wedges
- Fresh cilantro for garnish

Instructions:

1. **Prepare the Meat:**
    - In a large pot or Dutch oven, heat the vegetable oil over medium-high heat. Add the chicken, beef, and pork. Brown the meat on all sides, about 5-7 minutes. You may need to do this in batches if your pot is not large enough.
2. **Build the Flavor Base:**
    - Remove the meat from the pot and set aside. In the same pot, add the chopped onion, garlic, tomato, and green bell pepper. Sauté until the vegetables are softened, about 5 minutes.
3. **Add Spices and Broth:**

- Stir in the bay leaves, ground cumin, paprika, oregano, salt, and black pepper. Cook for another minute to toast the spices.
- Return the browned meat to the pot. Pour in the beef or chicken broth and bring to a boil. Reduce heat and simmer for 30 minutes.

4. **Add Vegetables:**
   - Add the potatoes, carrots, plantain, yuca, and corn to the pot. Continue to simmer for 30-40 minutes, or until the meat is tender and the vegetables are cooked through.

5. **Finish and Serve:**
   - Stir in the chopped cilantro and adjust seasoning with additional salt and pepper if needed.
   - Serve the Sancocho hot over a bed of cooked white rice. Accompany with slices of avocado, lime wedges, and additional fresh cilantro if desired.

Tips:

- **Meat Variations:** You can adjust the types and cuts of meat based on your preference. Some variations include using just one type of meat or adding additional cuts.
- **Vegetables:** If you can't find yuca, you can substitute with more potatoes or other root vegetables. Plantains can be substituted with sweet potatoes if desired.

Storage:

- **Refrigeration:** Leftover Sancocho can be stored in an airtight container in the refrigerator for up to 4 days.
- **Freezing:** Sancocho freezes well. Store in a freezer-safe container for up to 2-3 months. Thaw in the refrigerator before reheating.

Enjoy this delicious and comforting Colombian Sancocho, a dish that's perfect for feeding a crowd and enjoying a taste of Colombian culture!

Uruguayan Tortas Fritas

Ingredients:

- 2 cups all-purpose flour
- 1 tablespoon baking powder
- 1/2 teaspoon salt
- 2 tablespoons sugar
- 1/4 cup unsalted butter, cold and cut into small pieces
- 1 large egg
- 1/2 cup milk (more if needed)
- Vegetable oil, for frying
- Powdered sugar, for dusting (optional)

Instructions:

1. **Prepare the Dough:**
   - In a large bowl, whisk together the flour, baking powder, salt, and sugar.
   - Cut in the cold butter using a pastry cutter or your fingers until the mixture resembles coarse crumbs.
   - In a separate small bowl, whisk the egg and milk together. Add to the flour mixture and stir until a dough forms. If the dough is too dry, add a little more milk, one tablespoon at a time.
2. **Roll and Cut the Dough:**
   - Turn the dough out onto a lightly floured surface and knead gently for a minute or two until smooth.
   - Roll out the dough to about 1/8 inch (3 mm) thickness. Using a round cutter (about 3-4 inches in diameter) or a glass, cut out circles of dough. You can also cut the dough into squares or rectangles if preferred.
3. **Heat the Oil:**
   - Heat about 1-2 inches of vegetable oil in a large skillet or deep fryer over medium-high heat until it reaches 350°F (175°C). To test if the oil is hot enough, drop a small piece of dough into the oil; it should float and sizzle.
4. **Fry the Tortas Fritas:**
   - Carefully place a few pieces of dough into the hot oil, being careful not to overcrowd the pan. Fry for about 1-2 minutes on each side, or until golden brown and crispy.
   - Use a slotted spoon to remove the tortas fritas from the oil and drain on paper towels.
5. **Serve:**
   - While still warm, dust with powdered sugar if desired. Serve the tortas fritas on their own, or with a side of jam, honey, or dulce de leche.

Tips:

- **Oil Temperature:** Maintaining the correct oil temperature is crucial for achieving crispy tortas fritas. If the oil is too hot, they may brown too quickly on the outside while remaining raw inside. If it's too cool, they may become greasy.
- **Dough Consistency:** The dough should be soft but not sticky. If it's too sticky, add a little more flour. If too dry, add a bit more milk.

Storage:

- **Room Temperature:** Tortas fritas are best enjoyed fresh but can be stored at room temperature in an airtight container for up to 2 days.
- **Reheating:** To re-crisp, you can reheat them in a toaster oven or a conventional oven at 350°F (175°C) for about 5-7 minutes.

Enjoy these delightful Uruguayan Tortas Fritas, a simple yet delicious treat that's perfect for any time of day!

Venezuelan Cachapas

Ingredients:

- 2 cups fresh or frozen corn kernels (if using frozen, thaw them first)
- 1/2 cup milk
- 1/4 cup sugar
- 1/4 cup all-purpose flour
- 1/4 teaspoon baking powder
- 1/4 teaspoon salt
- 1 large egg
- 2 tablespoons butter, melted
- Additional butter or oil, for cooking

For Serving:

- Queso de Mano or any soft, mild cheese (like mozzarella or queso fresco)
- Butter or sour cream (optional)

Instructions:

1. **Prepare the Corn Mixture:**
   - In a blender or food processor, combine the corn kernels, milk, and sugar. Blend until smooth.
   - Add the flour, baking powder, salt, egg, and melted butter to the blender. Blend again until all ingredients are well combined and the mixture is smooth.
2. **Heat the Pan:**
   - Heat a non-stick skillet or griddle over medium heat. Lightly grease with butter or oil.
3. **Cook the Cachapas:**
   - Pour about 1/4 cup of the corn batter onto the skillet for each cachapa. Use the back of a spoon or a spatula to spread the batter into a round, even shape about 1/4 inch (6 mm) thick.
   - Cook for about 3-4 minutes on one side, until bubbles form on the surface and the edges look set. Flip and cook for another 2-3 minutes on the other side, until golden brown and cooked through.
   - Repeat with the remaining batter, adding more butter or oil to the skillet as needed.
4. **Serve:**
   - Serve the cachapas warm, topped with slices of queso de mano or other soft cheese. You can also spread with butter or sour cream if desired.

Tips:

- **Corn:** Fresh corn is best, but frozen corn works well too. Just make sure to thaw it completely before using.

- **Batter Consistency:** If the batter is too thick, you can add a little more milk to reach the desired consistency.

Storage:

- **Refrigeration:** Leftover cachapas can be stored in an airtight container in the refrigerator for up to 3 days.
- **Freezing:** You can freeze cooked cachapas by placing them between layers of parchment paper in a freezer-safe bag. Reheat in a skillet or oven to restore some of their crispiness.

Enjoy these delicious Venezuelan Cachapas, a sweet and savory treat that's a true taste of Venezuelan cuisine!

Ecuadorian Hornado

Ingredients:

For the Pork:

- 1 whole pork shoulder or pork leg (about 5-6 lbs), skin on
- 1 tablespoon vegetable oil
- 4 cloves garlic, minced
- 2 tablespoons achiote paste (or substitute with paprika and a bit of turmeric)
- 1 tablespoon ground cumin
- 1 tablespoon ground coriander
- 1 tablespoon dried oregano
- 1 teaspoon paprika
- 1 tablespoon salt
- 1 teaspoon black pepper
- 1 cup orange juice (freshly squeezed is best)
- 1 cup water
- 1 large onion, quartered
- 2 bay leaves

For Serving:

- 3-4 cups hominy (mote), cooked
- 2-3 plantains, peeled and sliced
- 1 large red onion, thinly sliced
- 1 large tomato, diced
- 1/4 cup fresh cilantro, chopped
- Lime wedges
- Salsa or hot sauce (optional)

Instructions:

1. **Prepare the Pork:**
    - Preheat your oven to 325°F (163°C).
    - In a small bowl, combine the minced garlic, achiote paste, ground cumin, ground coriander, dried oregano, paprika, salt, and black pepper to create a spice paste.
    - Rub the spice paste all over the pork, making sure to get some under the skin if possible.
    - Place the pork in a large roasting pan. Pour the orange juice and water around the pork. Add the quartered onion and bay leaves to the pan.
2. **Roast the Pork:**
    - Cover the roasting pan with aluminum foil.
    - Roast in the preheated oven for about 3 hours, or until the pork is tender. Remove the foil for the last 30 minutes to allow the skin to become crispy. If

needed, increase the oven temperature to 400°F (200°C) during the last 15 minutes to crisp the skin further.
- Baste the pork occasionally with the pan juices to keep it moist.
3. **Prepare the Accompaniments:**
    - While the pork is roasting, prepare the hominy according to package instructions if not using pre-cooked.
    - Slice the plantains and fry them in a pan with a bit of oil until golden and crispy, or bake them for a healthier option.
    - Prepare a simple salad with thinly sliced red onion, diced tomato, and chopped cilantro. Squeeze lime juice over the top.
4. **Serve:**
    - Once the pork is done, let it rest for 10-15 minutes before carving.
    - Serve the hornado with the cooked hominy, fried plantains, and the fresh salad on the side.
    - Garnish with lime wedges and additional salsa or hot sauce if desired.

Tips:

- **Crispy Skin:** If the skin is not as crispy as you'd like, you can use a broiler for a few minutes to achieve the desired crispiness. Watch it closely to prevent burning.
- **Flavor Variations:** You can adjust the spices to your taste. Adding a bit of chili powder or hot sauce to the marinade can add extra heat if desired.

Storage:

- **Refrigeration:** Leftover hornado can be stored in an airtight container in the refrigerator for up to 4 days.
- **Freezing:** You can freeze leftover pork in a freezer-safe container for up to 2-3 months. Thaw in the refrigerator before reheating.

Enjoy your Ecuadorian Hornado, a flavorful and hearty dish that showcases the rich culinary traditions of Ecuador!

Bolivian Silpancho

Ingredients:

For the Beef:

- 1 lb (450 g) beef round or sirloin, thinly sliced
- 1 cup all-purpose flour
- 1 cup breadcrumbs
- 1 teaspoon paprika
- 1/2 teaspoon ground cumin
- 1/2 teaspoon garlic powder
- Salt and black pepper to taste
- 2 large eggs, beaten
- Vegetable oil, for frying

For the Rice:

- 2 cups long-grain rice
- 4 cups water
- 1 tablespoon vegetable oil
- 1 teaspoon salt

For the Potatoes:

- 4 medium potatoes, peeled and cut into thin rounds
- Vegetable oil, for frying
- Salt, to taste

For the Salad:

- 2 large tomatoes, diced
- 1 large red onion, thinly sliced
- 1 cucumber, peeled and diced
- 1/4 cup fresh cilantro, chopped
- 2 tablespoons olive oil
- 1 tablespoon red wine vinegar or lime juice
- Salt and black pepper to taste

Instructions:

1. **Prepare the Beef:**
   - Place the beef slices between two sheets of plastic wrap or parchment paper. Pound the beef with a meat mallet or rolling pin until thin and even.

- Set up a breading station: Place flour in one shallow dish, beaten eggs in another, and a mixture of breadcrumbs, paprika, cumin, garlic powder, salt, and pepper in a third dish.
- Dredge each beef slice in flour, shaking off the excess. Dip in the beaten eggs, then coat with the breadcrumb mixture, pressing lightly to adhere.

2. **Cook the Beef:**
   - Heat vegetable oil in a large skillet over medium-high heat.
   - Fry the breaded beef slices in the hot oil until golden brown and cooked through, about 3-4 minutes per side. Remove from the skillet and drain on paper towels.

3. **Prepare the Rice:**
   - Rinse the rice under cold water until the water runs clear.
   - In a medium saucepan, heat the vegetable oil over medium heat. Add the rice and cook, stirring occasionally, until the rice is slightly toasted, about 2-3 minutes.
   - Add the water and salt, bring to a boil, then reduce heat to low, cover, and simmer for 15-20 minutes, or until the rice is cooked and the water is absorbed. Fluff with a fork before serving.

4. **Prepare the Potatoes:**
   - Heat vegetable oil in a large skillet over medium-high heat.
   - Fry the potato rounds in batches until golden brown and crispy, about 3-4 minutes per side. Drain on paper towels and season with salt.

5. **Prepare the Salad:**
   - In a large bowl, combine the diced tomatoes, sliced red onion, diced cucumber, and chopped cilantro.
   - Drizzle with olive oil and red wine vinegar or lime juice. Season with salt and black pepper to taste. Toss to combine.

6. **Serve:**
   - On each plate, place a serving of rice and a few potato rounds.
   - Top with a fried beef slice and serve with the fresh salad on the side.

Tips:

- **Beef:** If the beef slices are tough, you can marinate them in a bit of soy sauce and lime juice to tenderize.
- **Crispy Potatoes:** Ensure the oil is hot enough before frying to achieve crispy potatoes. Avoid overcrowding the pan to maintain the oil temperature.

Storage:

- **Refrigeration:** Store leftovers in an airtight container in the refrigerator for up to 3 days.
- **Freezing:** Freeze cooked beef and potatoes in a freezer-safe container for up to 2 months. Reheat in the oven or skillet for best results.

Enjoy your Bolivian Silpancho, a satisfying and flavorful dish that captures the essence of Bolivian cuisine!

Paraguayan Mbejú

Ingredients:

- 2 cups cassava flour (also known as yuca flour)
- 1 cup grated cheese (Paraguayan cheese, or use a mix of mozzarella and Parmesan if unavailable)
- 1/2 cup unsalted butter, melted
- 1/2 cup milk
- 1/2 teaspoon baking powder
- 1/2 teaspoon salt
- 1/4 teaspoon black pepper
- 1 large egg (optional, for added richness)

Instructions:

1. **Preheat the Pan:**
    - Heat a large skillet or griddle over medium heat. You do not need to add oil as the Mbejú will be cooked in its own fat.
2. **Prepare the Dough:**
    - In a large bowl, combine the cassava flour, grated cheese, baking powder, salt, and black pepper.
    - Add the melted butter and mix until the mixture resembles coarse crumbs.
    - Gradually add the milk and mix until the dough comes together. If using, beat the egg and mix it into the dough for a richer texture. The dough should be slightly crumbly but able to hold together when pressed.
3. **Cook the Mbejú:**
    - Take small portions of the dough and flatten them into rounds about 1/4 inch (6 mm) thick. You can use your hands or a rolling pin for this.
    - Place the rounds onto the preheated skillet or griddle. Cook for about 4-5 minutes on each side, or until golden brown and crispy. You can adjust the heat as necessary to avoid burning.
4. **Serve:**
    - Once cooked, transfer the Mbejú to a plate lined with paper towels to absorb any excess fat.
    - Serve warm, as is, or with your favorite dipping sauce or accompaniment.

Tips:

- **Cassava Flour:** Make sure you're using cassava flour (yuca flour) and not tapioca flour, as they are different products. Cassava flour provides the authentic texture and flavor for Mbejú.
- **Cheese:** Paraguayan cheese has a unique flavor and texture, but if it's not available, a mix of mozzarella and Parmesan can be used as a substitute.

Storage:

- **Room Temperature:** Mbejú is best enjoyed fresh but can be stored at room temperature for up to 2 days in an airtight container.
- **Refrigeration:** Store leftovers in the refrigerator for up to 5 days. Reheat in a skillet or toaster oven to restore some of the crispiness.

Enjoy your delicious Paraguayan Mbejú, a simple yet delightful treat that showcases the flavors of Paraguay!

Brazilian Coxinhas

Ingredients:

For the Filling:

- 1 lb (450 g) chicken breast, boneless and skinless
- 1 medium onion, finely chopped
- 3 cloves garlic, minced
- 1/2 cup diced tomatoes (fresh or canned)
- 1/4 cup chopped parsley
- 1/4 cup chopped green olives (optional)
- 1 tablespoon olive oil
- 1 teaspoon paprika
- 1/2 teaspoon ground cumin
- Salt and black pepper to taste

For the Dough:

- 2 cups all-purpose flour
- 1 cup chicken broth (homemade or store-bought)
- 1/4 cup unsalted butter
- 1/2 teaspoon salt
- 1/2 teaspoon baking powder

For Breading and Frying:

- 1 cup all-purpose flour (for dredging)
- 2 large eggs, beaten
- 2 cups breadcrumbs (panko or regular)
- Vegetable oil, for frying

Instructions:

1. **Prepare the Filling:**
     - In a large pot, bring water to a boil and cook the chicken breasts until fully cooked, about 15-20 minutes. Remove the chicken from the pot and let it cool slightly. Shred the chicken into small pieces using two forks.
     - In a large skillet, heat olive oil over medium heat. Add the chopped onion and garlic, and cook until translucent.
     - Add the diced tomatoes, parsley, olives (if using), paprika, cumin, salt, and pepper. Cook for a few minutes until the tomatoes start to break down.
     - Stir in the shredded chicken and cook for an additional 5 minutes, allowing the flavors to meld. Remove from heat and let it cool.
2. **Prepare the Dough:**

- In a medium saucepan, heat the chicken broth and butter until the butter is melted and the broth is warm.
- In a large mixing bowl, combine the flour, salt, and baking powder.
- Gradually pour the warm broth mixture into the flour mixture, stirring continuously until a smooth dough forms. Knead the dough for a few minutes until it becomes soft and pliable.

3. **Assemble the Coxinhas:**
   - Take a small piece of dough (about the size of a golf ball) and flatten it into a circle using your hands or a rolling pin. Place a small spoonful of the chicken filling in the center.
   - Fold the edges of the dough over the filling and shape it into a teardrop or drumstick shape, pinching the edges to seal. Ensure that the filling is completely enclosed.

4. **Bread the Coxinhas:**
   - Dredge each coxinha in flour, shaking off the excess.
   - Dip into the beaten eggs, allowing any excess to drip off.
   - Coat with breadcrumbs, pressing gently to adhere.

5. **Fry the Coxinhas:**
   - Heat vegetable oil in a deep fryer or large skillet over medium-high heat to 350°F (175°C).
   - Fry the coxinhas in batches, being careful not to overcrowd the pan. Cook until golden brown and crispy, about 3-4 minutes per side.
   - Remove with a slotted spoon and drain on paper towels.

6. **Serve:**
   - Serve the coxinhas warm, as an appetizer or snack. They pair well with a variety of dipping sauces or just on their own.

Tips:

- **Filling Variations:** You can add cheese or other ingredients to the chicken filling for extra flavor.
- **Dough Consistency:** The dough should be soft but not sticky. If it's too sticky, add a little more flour. If it's too dry, add a bit more chicken broth.

Storage:

- **Refrigeration:** Leftover coxinhas can be stored in an airtight container in the refrigerator for up to 3 days.
- **Freezing:** Freeze uncooked coxinhas on a baking sheet until firm, then transfer to a freezer-safe bag. Fry from frozen, adding a few extra minutes to the cooking time.

Enjoy your delicious Brazilian Coxinhas, a delightful and savory treat that captures the essence of Brazilian cuisine!

Argentinian Provoleta

Ingredients:

- 1 large round of provolone cheese (about 8 oz or 225 g)
- 1-2 tablespoons olive oil
- 1 teaspoon dried oregano
- 1/2 teaspoon crushed red pepper flakes (optional)
- Freshly ground black pepper, to taste
- Fresh parsley, chopped (for garnish, optional)
- Crusty bread or baguette, for serving

Instructions:

1. **Prepare the Grill or Oven:**
   - **Grill:** Preheat your grill to medium heat.
   - **Oven:** Preheat your oven to 375°F (190°C).
2. **Prepare the Cheese:**
   - Lightly brush a grill-safe skillet or an oven-proof dish with olive oil.
   - Place the provolone cheese in the skillet or dish.
3. **Season the Cheese:**
   - Drizzle the cheese with olive oil.
   - Sprinkle with dried oregano, crushed red pepper flakes (if using), and freshly ground black pepper.
4. **Cook the Cheese:**
   - **On the Grill:** Place the skillet on the grill. Close the lid and cook for about 5-7 minutes, or until the cheese is melted and bubbly. Keep an eye on it to prevent burning.
   - **In the Oven:** Place the dish on the middle rack of the oven. Bake for 10-15 minutes, or until the cheese is melted and starting to brown.
5. **Garnish and Serve:**
   - Remove the cheese from the heat.
   - Garnish with chopped fresh parsley, if desired.
   - Serve immediately with crusty bread or baguette slices for dipping.

Tips:

- **Cheese Quality:** Use a good-quality provolone cheese for the best flavor. If provolone is not available, other semi-hard cheeses with good melting qualities can be used, but provolone is traditional.
- **Serving:** Provoleta is best enjoyed hot and gooey, so serve it right away.

Storage:

- **Leftovers:** Store any leftovers in an airtight container in the refrigerator for up to 2 days. Reheat gently in the oven or microwave before serving to maintain its melted texture.

Enjoy your delicious Argentinian Provoleta, a simple yet indulgent treat that perfectly captures the essence of Argentine cuisine!

Chilean Cazuela

Ingredients:

- **For the Broth:**
    - 2 lbs (900 g) beef shank or bone-in chicken thighs
    - 8 cups water
    - 1 onion, quartered
    - 2 cloves garlic, peeled
    - 1 bay leaf
    - 1 teaspoon dried oregano
    - Salt and black pepper to taste
- **For the Stew:**
    - 2 tablespoons vegetable oil
    - 1 onion, chopped
    - 2 cloves garlic, minced
    - 2 carrots, peeled and sliced
    - 2 potatoes, peeled and cut into large chunks
    - 1 cup pumpkin or butternut squash, peeled and cut into chunks
    - 1/2 cup green beans or peas
    - 1/2 cup corn kernels (fresh or frozen)
    - 1 tomato, diced
    - 1/4 cup fresh cilantro, chopped
    - 1 teaspoon ground cumin
    - 1 teaspoon paprika
    - 1/2 teaspoon ground chili powder (optional, for a bit of heat)
- **For Garnish (Optional):**
    - Fresh cilantro, chopped
    - Lime wedges

Instructions:

1. **Prepare the Broth:**
    - In a large pot, add the beef shank or chicken, water, onion, garlic, bay leaf, oregano, salt, and pepper.
    - Bring to a boil, then reduce heat to low. Simmer for about 1.5 to 2 hours, until the meat is tender and the broth is flavorful.
    - Remove the meat from the pot and set aside. Strain the broth to remove solids and return it to the pot.
2. **Prepare the Stew:**
    - Heat vegetable oil in a large skillet over medium heat. Add the chopped onion and garlic, and cook until softened.
    - Add the diced tomato, cumin, paprika, and chili powder (if using). Cook for an additional 5 minutes until the tomatoes have broken down.
3. **Add Vegetables:**

- Add the carrots, potatoes, pumpkin, and green beans (or peas) to the pot with the broth.
- Simmer for about 20-30 minutes, or until the vegetables are tender.
4. **Add Meat and Corn:**
   - Return the cooked meat to the pot along with the corn kernels. Simmer for an additional 10 minutes to heat through and meld the flavors.
5. **Season and Garnish:**
   - Adjust seasoning with salt and pepper as needed.
   - Stir in fresh cilantro just before serving.
6. **Serve:**
   - Ladle the cazuela into bowls, ensuring each serving gets a good mix of meat and vegetables.
   - Garnish with additional fresh cilantro and serve with lime wedges on the side for an extra burst of flavor.

Tips:

- **Meat Choice:** Beef shank adds richness and flavor, but chicken thighs are a lighter alternative. You can also use a combination of both.
- **Vegetables:** Feel free to adjust the vegetables based on what's in season or available. Other additions like bell peppers or celery can also be included.

Storage:

- **Refrigeration:** Cazuela can be stored in an airtight container in the refrigerator for up to 4 days.
- **Freezing:** It freezes well in an airtight container for up to 3 months. Reheat thoroughly before serving.

Enjoy your comforting and flavorful Chilean Cazuela, a dish that truly embodies the essence of Chilean cuisine!

Peruvian Causa Limeña

Ingredients:

For the Potato Mixture:

- 2 lbs (900 g) Peruvian yellow potatoes or other yellow-fleshed potatoes
- 2-3 tablespoons aji amarillo paste (available at Latin American markets or online) or substitute with a mixture of yellow bell pepper and a touch of hot sauce
- 1/4 cup freshly squeezed lime juice
- 1/4 cup vegetable oil
- Salt to taste

For the Filling:

- **Chicken Filling:**
    - 2 cups cooked, shredded chicken (preferably from boiled chicken breast)
    - 1/2 cup mayonnaise
    - 1/4 cup chopped fresh cilantro
    - 1/4 cup finely diced red onion
    - 1/4 cup diced red bell pepper
    - Salt and pepper to taste
- **Alternative Fillings:**
    - **Tuna Filling:** Use 1 can of tuna (drained) mixed with 1/4 cup mayonnaise, 1/4 cup chopped fresh cilantro, 1/4 cup diced red onion, and 1/4 cup diced green olives. Season with salt and pepper.
    - **Vegetable Filling:** Mix 1 cup diced avocado, 1/2 cup diced tomatoes, and 1/2 cup sliced olives with a squeeze of lime juice.

For Garnish (Optional):

- Fresh parsley or cilantro, chopped
- Lime wedges
- Slices of avocado
- Hard-boiled eggs, sliced
- Olives

Instructions:

1. **Prepare the Potatoes:**
    - Boil the potatoes in a large pot of salted water until tender, about 20-25 minutes. Drain and let them cool slightly.
    - Peel the potatoes while still warm and mash them until smooth. You can use a potato ricer for a finer texture.
2. **Season the Potato Mixture:**

- In a large bowl, mix the mashed potatoes with aji amarillo paste, lime juice, vegetable oil, and salt. Adjust the seasoning to taste. The mixture should be smooth and slightly tangy.
3. **Prepare the Filling:**
    - **Chicken Filling:** In a separate bowl, combine the shredded chicken, mayonnaise, chopped cilantro, diced red onion, and diced red bell pepper. Season with salt and pepper. Mix well.
    - Alternatively, prepare your chosen filling if using tuna or vegetables.
4. **Assemble the Causa:**
    - Use a mold or a springform pan to shape the causa. Press a layer of the seasoned potato mixture into the bottom of the mold to create the base layer.
    - Add a layer of the filling (chicken, tuna, or vegetables) on top of the potato base.
    - Spread another layer of the seasoned potato mixture over the filling, smoothing it out with a spatula.
    - Chill the assembled causa in the refrigerator for at least 1 hour to allow the flavors to meld and the layers to set.
5. **Serve:**
    - Remove the causa from the mold and transfer it to a serving platter.
    - Garnish with fresh parsley or cilantro, lime wedges, and optional slices of avocado, hard-boiled eggs, or olives.

Tips:

- **Aji Amarillo Paste:** If aji amarillo paste is not available, you can make a substitute by blending yellow bell peppers with a bit of hot sauce, though the flavor will differ slightly.
- **Mold:** If you don't have a mold, you can layer the causa in a dish and cut it into squares or slices.

Storage:

- **Refrigeration:** Causa Limeña can be stored in the refrigerator for up to 3 days. It's best served cold or at room temperature.

Enjoy your Causa Limeña, a delightful Peruvian dish that showcases the rich flavors and textures of traditional Peruvian cuisine!

Colombian Arroz con Coco

Ingredients:

- 1 cup long-grain white rice
- 1 can (13.5 oz) coconut milk (full-fat for best flavor)
- 1 cup water
- 1/4 cup sugar (adjust to taste)
- 1/2 teaspoon salt
- 1 cinnamon stick (optional)
- 1/2 cup shredded coconut (sweetened or unsweetened)
- 2 tablespoons vegetable oil or butter
- 1/4 cup raisins (optional, for added sweetness)
- 1/4 cup chopped fresh cilantro or scallions (for garnish, optional)

Instructions:

1. **Rinse the Rice:**
   - Rinse the rice under cold water until the water runs clear. This removes excess starch and helps prevent the rice from being too sticky.
2. **Cook the Rice:**
   - In a medium saucepan, heat the vegetable oil or butter over medium heat. Add the rinsed rice and cook for 2-3 minutes, stirring frequently, until the rice is lightly toasted.
3. **Prepare the Coconut Mixture:**
   - In a separate bowl, mix the coconut milk, water, sugar, and salt. Stir until the sugar is dissolved. If using, add the cinnamon stick for extra flavor.
4. **Combine and Cook:**
   - Pour the coconut mixture over the toasted rice in the saucepan. Stir to combine.
   - Bring the mixture to a boil, then reduce the heat to low. Cover the saucepan with a tight-fitting lid and simmer for about 15-20 minutes, or until the rice is tender and the liquid is absorbed.
5. **Add Shredded Coconut and Raisins:**
   - If using, stir in the shredded coconut and raisins. Cover and let the rice sit for an additional 5 minutes off the heat to allow the flavors to meld.
6. **Garnish and Serve:**
   - Remove the cinnamon stick, if used.
   - Fluff the rice with a fork and garnish with chopped fresh cilantro or scallions, if desired.
   - Serve warm as a side dish with your favorite main course.

Tips:

- **Rice Choice:** Use long-grain white rice for the best texture. Short-grain or jasmine rice can also be used, but may alter the final texture slightly.

- **Sweetness Level:** Adjust the amount of sugar to your taste. Some people prefer a sweeter dish, while others might like it less sweet.
- **Coconut Milk:** Full-fat coconut milk provides a richer flavor and creamier texture. If you prefer a lighter version, you can use light coconut milk or a combination of coconut milk and low-fat milk.

Storage:

- **Refrigeration:** Leftover Arroz con Coco can be stored in an airtight container in the refrigerator for up to 4 days.
- **Freezing:** It can be frozen for up to 2 months. Reheat gently, adding a little water or coconut milk if needed to restore creaminess.

Enjoy your Colombian Arroz con Coco, a delightful and creamy rice dish that's sure to add a touch of Colombian flavor to your meal!

Uruguayan Empanadas de Carne

Ingredients:

For the Filling:

- 1 lb (450 g) ground beef
- 1 tablespoon vegetable oil
- 1 medium onion, finely chopped
- 2 cloves garlic, minced
- 1/2 cup green olives, pitted and chopped
- 1/2 cup raisins (optional, for a touch of sweetness)
- 1 hard-boiled egg, chopped
- 1 teaspoon ground cumin
- 1 teaspoon smoked paprika
- 1/2 teaspoon dried oregano
- Salt and black pepper to taste
- 1/4 cup fresh parsley or cilantro, chopped

For the Dough:

- 2 1/2 cups all-purpose flour
- 1/2 cup unsalted butter, cold and cubed
- 1/2 teaspoon salt
- 1 large egg
- 1/4 cup cold water (more if needed)

For Assembly:

- 1 egg, beaten (for egg wash)
- Additional flour for rolling

Instructions:

1. **Prepare the Filling:**
    - Heat the vegetable oil in a large skillet over medium heat. Add the chopped onion and cook until softened, about 5 minutes.
    - Add the minced garlic and cook for an additional minute.
    - Add the ground beef to the skillet and cook until browned, breaking it up with a spoon as it cooks. Drain any excess fat if necessary.
    - Stir in the chopped olives, raisins (if using), and chopped hard-boiled egg.
    - Season with ground cumin, smoked paprika, dried oregano, salt, and pepper. Mix well and cook for an additional 5 minutes.
    - Stir in the chopped parsley or cilantro and remove from heat. Let the filling cool before using.
2. **Prepare the Dough:**

- In a large bowl, mix the flour and salt. Add the cold, cubed butter and use a pastry cutter or your fingers to work it into the flour until the mixture resembles coarse crumbs.
- In a small bowl, beat the egg and add it to the flour mixture. Stir until combined.
- Gradually add cold water, one tablespoon at a time, until the dough comes together. You may need more or less water, so add it slowly.
- Turn the dough out onto a floured surface and knead lightly until smooth. Wrap the dough in plastic wrap and refrigerate for at least 30 minutes.

3. **Assemble the Empanadas:**
   - Preheat your oven to 375°F (190°C) and line a baking sheet with parchment paper.
   - On a floured surface, roll out the dough to about 1/8 inch (3 mm) thickness. Use a round cutter (about 4-5 inches in diameter) to cut out circles of dough.
   - Place a spoonful of the cooled filling in the center of each dough circle. Fold the dough over to form a half-moon shape and press the edges together to seal. You can crimp the edges with a fork or fold them over for a more decorative finish.
   - Place the empanadas on the prepared baking sheet and brush the tops with the beaten egg.

4. **Bake:**
   - Bake the empanadas in the preheated oven for 20-25 minutes, or until they are golden brown and crispy.

5. **Serve:**
   - Let the empanadas cool slightly before serving. Enjoy them warm or at room temperature.

Tips:

- **Dough:** For an extra flaky texture, make sure the butter is very cold and handle the dough as little as possible.
- **Filling:** You can customize the filling by adding other ingredients like sautéed mushrooms or bell peppers.

Storage:

- **Refrigeration:** Store leftover empanadas in an airtight container in the refrigerator for up to 3 days.
- **Freezing:** Empanadas can be frozen before baking. Place them on a baking sheet and freeze until solid, then transfer to a freezer bag. Bake from frozen, adding a few extra minutes to the baking time.

Enjoy your Uruguayan Empanadas de Carne, a delicious and satisfying treat that showcases the flavors of Uruguay!

Venezuelan Tequeños

Ingredients:

For the Dough:

- 2 1/2 cups all-purpose flour
- 1/2 teaspoon salt
- 1/2 cup unsalted butter, cold and cubed
- 1 large egg
- 1/2 cup cold water (more if needed)

For the Filling:

- 8 oz (225 g) white cheese (such as queso blanco, mozzarella, or any melting cheese)
- 1 egg (for egg wash, optional)

For Frying:

- Vegetable oil (for deep frying)

Instructions:

1. **Prepare the Dough:**
   - In a large bowl, combine the flour and salt. Add the cold, cubed butter and use a pastry cutter or your fingers to work it into the flour until the mixture resembles coarse crumbs.
   - In a small bowl, beat the egg and add it to the flour mixture. Stir until combined.
   - Gradually add cold water, one tablespoon at a time, until the dough comes together. You may need more or less water, so add it slowly.
   - Turn the dough out onto a floured surface and knead lightly until smooth. Wrap the dough in plastic wrap and refrigerate for at least 30 minutes.
2. **Prepare the Filling:**
   - Cut the cheese into sticks about 1/2 inch (1.3 cm) thick. If using mozzarella, you can cut it into strips or sticks.
3. **Assemble the Tequeños:**
   - On a floured surface, roll out the dough to about 1/8 inch (3 mm) thickness. Cut the dough into rectangles large enough to wrap around the cheese sticks.
   - Place a cheese stick on one end of each rectangle and roll it up, sealing the edges as you go. Make sure the cheese is fully enclosed and the ends are sealed well to prevent leaking during frying.
   - If desired, brush the edges with a beaten egg for extra sealing and browning.
4. **Fry the Tequeños:**
   - Heat vegetable oil in a deep skillet or pot to 350°F (175°C). There should be enough oil to submerge the tequeños.

- Fry the tequeños in batches, making sure not to overcrowd the pan. Cook until they are golden brown and crispy, about 2-3 minutes per batch.
- Use a slotted spoon to remove the tequeños from the oil and place them on paper towels to drain.

5. **Serve:**
    - Serve the tequeños warm with your favorite dipping sauces. They pair well with guasacaca (Venezuelan avocado sauce), salsa, or a simple tomato ketchup.

Tips:

- **Cheese:** For the best results, use cheese that melts well and has a mild flavor. Queso blanco, mozzarella, or even cheddar can work, but mozzarella is often preferred for its melting quality.
- **Dough:** Make sure the dough is well-chilled before rolling out to prevent it from becoming too sticky.

Storage:

- **Refrigeration:** Store leftover tequeños in an airtight container in the refrigerator for up to 3 days. Reheat in a 350°F (175°C) oven for a few minutes to restore crispiness.
- **Freezing:** To freeze, place the assembled but uncooked tequeños on a baking sheet and freeze until solid. Transfer to a freezer bag and store for up to 2 months. Fry from frozen, adding a few extra minutes to the cooking time.

Enjoy your Venezuelan Tequeños, a delicious and crispy treat that's sure to be a hit at any gathering!

Ecuadorian Seco de Pollo

Ingredients:

For the Marinade:

- 1 whole chicken (about 3-4 lbs), cut into pieces
- 1 tablespoon ground cumin
- 1 tablespoon paprika
- 1 teaspoon garlic powder
- 1 teaspoon onion powder
- 1 teaspoon dried oregano
- 1 teaspoon salt
- 1/2 teaspoon black pepper
- Juice of 1 lime

For the Stew:

- 2 tablespoons vegetable oil
- 1 large onion, finely chopped
- 2 cloves garlic, minced
- 1 large bell pepper, chopped (red or green)
- 2 medium tomatoes, chopped
- 1/2 cup tomato paste
- 1 cup beer or chicken broth (or use water)
- 1 cup fresh cilantro, chopped
- 1-2 tablespoons aji amarillo paste (optional, for added heat)
- 1 teaspoon ground cumin
- 1 teaspoon paprika
- 1/2 teaspoon dried oregano
- Salt and black pepper to taste

For Garnish (Optional):

- Fresh cilantro, chopped
- Lime wedges

Instructions:

1. **Marinate the Chicken:**
    - In a large bowl, mix together the ground cumin, paprika, garlic powder, onion powder, dried oregano, salt, pepper, and lime juice. Rub this mixture all over the chicken pieces. Cover and refrigerate for at least 1 hour, or overnight for best results.
2. **Prepare the Stew:**
    - Heat the vegetable oil in a large pot or Dutch oven over medium heat.

- Add the chopped onion and cook until translucent, about 5 minutes.
- Add the minced garlic and chopped bell pepper, and cook for another 2 minutes.
- Stir in the chopped tomatoes and cook until they begin to break down, about 5 minutes.
- Add the tomato paste and cook for an additional 2 minutes, stirring frequently.

3. **Cook the Chicken:**
    - Add the marinated chicken pieces to the pot. Cook until they are browned on all sides, about 10 minutes.
    - Pour in the beer or chicken broth, and add the cilantro, aji amarillo paste (if using), ground cumin, paprika, dried oregano, salt, and black pepper.
    - Bring the mixture to a boil, then reduce the heat to low. Cover and simmer for about 30-40 minutes, or until the chicken is cooked through and tender.

4. **Finish and Serve:**
    - Once the chicken is cooked, taste the sauce and adjust the seasoning if necessary.
    - If the sauce is too thin, you can simmer uncovered for a few more minutes to reduce it to your desired consistency.

5. **Garnish and Serve:**
    - Garnish with fresh cilantro and serve with lime wedges on the side.
    - **Accompaniments:** Seco de Pollo is traditionally served with white rice and fried plantains. You can also serve it with avocado slices and a side salad.

Tips:

- **Aji Amarillo Paste:** If you can't find aji amarillo paste, you can substitute with a bit of hot sauce, though the flavor will be different.
- **Beer:** The beer adds depth to the stew, but you can use chicken broth or water as an alternative.

Storage:

- **Refrigeration:** Leftover Seco de Pollo can be stored in an airtight container in the refrigerator for up to 3 days.
- **Freezing:** It can be frozen for up to 2 months. Thaw in the refrigerator before reheating. Reheat thoroughly before serving.

Enjoy your Ecuadorian Seco de Pollo, a comforting and flavorful dish that captures the essence of Ecuadorian cuisine!

Bolivian Sopa de Maní

Ingredients:

- **For the Soup Base:**
    - 1 cup raw peanuts (unsalted)
    - 1 tablespoon vegetable oil
    - 1 medium onion, finely chopped
    - 2 cloves garlic, minced
    - 2 medium carrots, peeled and diced
    - 2 medium potatoes, peeled and diced
    - 1 bell pepper, chopped (red or green)
    - 1 cup cooked chicken, shredded (optional) or 1 cup beef, cubed (optional)
    - 4 cups chicken broth or water
    - 1 tablespoon tomato paste
    - 1 teaspoon ground cumin
    - 1 teaspoon paprika
    - 1 teaspoon dried oregano
    - Salt and black pepper to taste
- **For Garnish (Optional):**
    - Fresh cilantro or parsley, chopped
    - Lime wedges
    - Sliced avocado
    - Cooked rice or quinoa (optional)

Instructions:

1. **Prepare the Peanuts:**
    - Toast the raw peanuts in a dry skillet over medium heat until golden brown and fragrant, about 5 minutes. Let them cool slightly.
    - Once cooled, grind the peanuts in a food processor or blender until they form a coarse paste. Set aside.
2. **Cook the Soup Base:**
    - Heat the vegetable oil in a large pot over medium heat. Add the chopped onion and cook until translucent, about 5 minutes.
    - Add the minced garlic and cook for another minute.
    - Stir in the diced carrots, potatoes, and bell pepper. Cook for about 5 minutes, stirring occasionally.
    - If using meat, add the shredded chicken or cubed beef to the pot and cook for an additional 5 minutes.
3. **Add the Peanut Paste:**
    - Stir in the ground peanut paste, making sure it's well combined with the vegetables and meat.
    - Add the tomato paste, ground cumin, paprika, dried oregano, salt, and black pepper. Stir well.

4. **Simmer the Soup:**
    - Pour in the chicken broth or water, and bring the mixture to a boil.
    - Reduce the heat to low and let the soup simmer, covered, for about 20-30 minutes, or until the vegetables are tender and the flavors have melded.
5. **Blend (Optional):**
    - For a smoother texture, you can use an immersion blender to partially blend the soup, leaving some chunks for texture. Alternatively, blend a portion of the soup in a regular blender and return it to the pot.
6. **Serve:**
    - Ladle the soup into bowls and garnish with fresh cilantro or parsley, lime wedges, and slices of avocado if desired.
    - Serve with cooked rice or quinoa on the side, if you like.

Tips:

- **Peanut Paste:** The consistency of the peanut paste can be adjusted depending on how creamy you want the soup to be. You can add more peanuts if you like a richer flavor.
- **Meat:** If you prefer a vegetarian version, you can omit the meat and use vegetable broth instead of chicken broth.

Storage:

- **Refrigeration:** Store leftover Sopa de Maní in an airtight container in the refrigerator for up to 4 days.
- **Freezing:** The soup can be frozen for up to 2 months. Thaw in the refrigerator overnight before reheating. Reheat thoroughly before serving.

Enjoy your Bolivian Sopa de Maní, a comforting and flavorful soup that brings a taste of Bolivia to your table!

Paraguayan Kivevé

Ingredients:

- 1 medium butternut squash or pumpkin, peeled, seeded, and diced
- 2 cups corn kernels (fresh, frozen, or canned)
- 1/2 cup chopped onions
- 2 cloves garlic, minced
- 1 bell pepper, chopped (red or green)
- 1/2 lb (225 g) pork or beef (optional), cut into small cubes
- 4 cups chicken broth or water
- 2 tablespoons vegetable oil
- 1 teaspoon ground cumin
- 1 teaspoon paprika
- 1/2 teaspoon dried oregano
- Salt and black pepper to taste
- 1 tablespoon fresh parsley or cilantro, chopped (optional, for garnish)

Instructions:

1. **Prepare the Ingredients:**
   - Peel, seed, and dice the butternut squash or pumpkin into bite-sized cubes. If using fresh corn, cut the kernels off the cob.
2. **Cook the Meat (Optional):**
   - If using meat, heat the vegetable oil in a large pot over medium heat. Add the meat and cook until browned on all sides. Remove the meat and set it aside.
3. **Cook the Vegetables:**
   - In the same pot, add a little more oil if needed. Sauté the chopped onions until translucent, about 5 minutes.
   - Add the minced garlic and chopped bell pepper, and cook for another 2 minutes.
4. **Combine and Simmer:**
   - Return the cooked meat to the pot, if using. Add the diced squash or pumpkin and corn kernels. Stir well.
   - Pour in the chicken broth or water. Add ground cumin, paprika, dried oregano, salt, and black pepper. Stir to combine.
5. **Simmer the Kivevé:**
   - Bring the mixture to a boil, then reduce the heat to low. Cover and let it simmer for about 30-40 minutes, or until the squash or pumpkin is tender and the flavors are well combined.
6. **Adjust Seasoning:**
   - Taste the Kivevé and adjust the seasoning if needed. If the stew is too thick, you can add a bit more broth or water.
7. **Serve:**
   - Ladle the Kivevé into bowls and garnish with fresh parsley or cilantro if desired. Serve warm.

Tips:

- **Squash:** You can use butternut squash, pumpkin, or any other type of winter squash that you prefer. The key is to use a squash that becomes tender and slightly sweet when cooked.
- **Corn:** If using frozen or canned corn, drain and rinse if necessary. Fresh corn will give the best flavor and texture.

Storage:

- **Refrigeration:** Leftover Kiveré can be stored in an airtight container in the refrigerator for up to 4 days.
- **Freezing:** The stew can be frozen for up to 2 months. Thaw in the refrigerator overnight and reheat thoroughly before serving.

Enjoy your Paraguayan Kiveré, a delightful and hearty dish that brings the flavors of Paraguay to your table!

Brazilian Feijão Tropeiro

Ingredients:

- **For the Beans:**
    - 2 cups dried black beans or carioca beans
    - 1 bay leaf
    - Salt to taste
- **For the Dish:**
    - 2 tablespoons vegetable oil
    - 1/2 lb (225 g) bacon, diced
    - 1/2 lb (225 g) pork sausage, sliced (optional)
    - 1 large onion, chopped
    - 3 cloves garlic, minced
    - 1 bell pepper, chopped (red or green)
    - 2 tomatoes, chopped
    - 1 cup manioc flour (farinha de mandioca)
    - 1/2 cup fresh parsley, chopped
    - 2-3 green onions, chopped
    - 2-3 eggs, beaten (optional)
    - 1 cup cooked bacon or sausage drippings (optional for added flavor)
    - Salt and black pepper to taste

Instructions:

1. **Prepare the Beans:**
    - Rinse the beans under cold water and soak them in a large bowl of water overnight. Drain and rinse again.
    - In a large pot, add the soaked beans and cover with fresh water. Add the bay leaf and a pinch of salt.
    - Bring to a boil, then reduce the heat and simmer until the beans are tender, about 1-1.5 hours. Drain and set aside.
2. **Cook the Meats:**
    - Heat the vegetable oil in a large skillet or sauté pan over medium heat.
    - Add the diced bacon and cook until crispy. Remove the bacon from the pan and set aside, leaving some of the drippings in the pan.
    - In the same pan, add the sliced sausage (if using) and cook until browned. Remove and set aside with the bacon.
3. **Prepare the Vegetables:**
    - In the same pan, add the chopped onion and cook until translucent, about 5 minutes.
    - Add the minced garlic and cook for another minute.
    - Stir in the chopped bell pepper and tomatoes. Cook until the vegetables are tender, about 5 minutes.
4. **Combine Ingredients:**

- Return the cooked bacon and sausage to the pan with the vegetables. Stir well to combine.
- Add the cooked beans to the pan and mix everything together.
- Stir in the manioc flour (farinha de mandioca) gradually, mixing well to incorporate. This will help thicken and bind the mixture together.
- Cook for an additional 5-10 minutes, stirring occasionally, until everything is heated through and the flavors are well combined. If using, add the cooked bacon or sausage drippings for extra flavor.

5. **Add Optional Ingredients:**
   - If desired, push the mixture to one side of the pan and pour the beaten eggs into the empty space. Scramble the eggs until cooked, then mix them into the rest of the dish.

6. **Finish and Serve:**
   - Stir in the fresh parsley and green onions. Taste and adjust the seasoning with salt and black pepper if needed.
   - Serve hot, and enjoy with rice and a side of sautéed greens or a fresh salad.

Tips:

- **Manioc Flour:** Manioc flour (farinha de mandioca) is a key ingredient that gives Feijão Tropeiro its distinctive texture. It's available in Latin American grocery stores or online.
- **Vegetarian Option:** You can make a vegetarian version by omitting the bacon and sausage and using vegetable oil instead of bacon drippings.

Storage:

- **Refrigeration:** Leftover Feijão Tropeiro can be stored in an airtight container in the refrigerator for up to 4 days.
- **Freezing:** The dish can be frozen for up to 2 months. Thaw in the refrigerator overnight and reheat thoroughly before serving.

Enjoy your Brazilian Feijão Tropeiro, a flavorful and satisfying dish that embodies the heart of Brazilian comfort food!

Argentinian Milanesa

Ingredients:

- **For the Meat and Seafood:**
    - 1 lb (450 g) pork ribs or pork shoulder, cut into chunks
    - 1 lb (450 g) beef stew meat, cut into chunks
    - 1 lb (450 g) chicken thighs or drumsticks
    - 1/2 lb (225 g) chorizo sausage, sliced
    - 1/2 lb (225 g) smoked sausage or kielbasa, sliced
    - 1/2 lb (225 g) mussels or clams, scrubbed and debearded (optional)
    - 1/2 lb (225 g) shrimp, peeled and deveined (optional)
- **For the Vegetables:**
    - 4-5 large potatoes, peeled and cut into chunks
    - 3 large carrots, peeled and cut into chunks
    - 1 large onion, chopped
    - 2 cloves garlic, minced
    - 1 bell pepper, chopped (red or green)
    - 1 cup corn kernels (fresh, frozen, or canned)
    - 2-3 large tomatoes, chopped
- **For the Broth and Seasoning:**
    - 6 cups chicken broth or water
    - 2 tablespoons paprika
    - 1 tablespoon ground cumin
    - 1 teaspoon dried oregano
    - 1 teaspoon dried thyme
    - Salt and black pepper to taste
    - 2 bay leaves
- **For Garnish (Optional):**
    - Fresh parsley or cilantro, chopped
    - Lime wedges

Instructions:

1. **Prepare the Meat and Seafood:**
    - In a large pot or Dutch oven, heat a little oil over medium heat. Brown the pork ribs, beef stew meat, and chicken pieces in batches, if necessary. Remove and set aside.
2. **Cook the Base:**
    - In the same pot, add a bit more oil if needed. Sauté the chopped onion and garlic until translucent, about 5 minutes.
    - Add the chopped bell pepper and cook for an additional 2 minutes.
3. **Combine Ingredients:**
    - Return the browned meat to the pot. Add the potatoes, carrots, corn kernels, and chopped tomatoes.

- Pour in the chicken broth or water, ensuring that there's enough liquid to cover the ingredients.
- Stir in the paprika, ground cumin, dried oregano, dried thyme, salt, black pepper, and bay leaves.

4. **Simmer the Curanto:**
   - Bring the mixture to a boil, then reduce the heat to low. Cover and simmer for about 45 minutes, or until the meat is tender and the vegetables are cooked through.

5. **Add Seafood (Optional):**
   - If using seafood, add the mussels or clams and shrimp during the last 10 minutes of cooking. Cook until the seafood is cooked through and the mussels or clams have opened.

6. **Finish and Serve:**
   - Remove the bay leaves. Taste and adjust the seasoning with additional salt and pepper if needed.
   - Serve hot, garnished with fresh parsley or cilantro and lime wedges on the side.

Tips:

- **Cooking Method:** Traditional Curanto is often cooked in a pit with hot stones, but this stovetop method provides a more accessible way to enjoy this classic dish.
- **Variations:** You can customize Curanto with other meats or seafood based on your preference or availability.

Storage:

- **Refrigeration:** Leftover Curanto can be stored in an airtight container in the refrigerator for up to 4 days.
- **Freezing:** The stew can be frozen for up to 2 months. Thaw in the refrigerator overnight and reheat thoroughly before serving.

Enjoy your **Chilean Curanto**, a flavorful and comforting stew that brings the taste of Chiloé to your table!

Peruvian Anticuchos

Ingredients:

- **For the Marinade:**
    - 1/2 cup red wine vinegar
    - 1/4 cup soy sauce
    - 3 tablespoons vegetable oil
    - 4 cloves garlic, minced
    - 2 tablespoons aji panca paste (Peruvian red chili paste) or substitute with mild chili paste
    - 1 tablespoon aji amarillo paste (Peruvian yellow chili paste) or substitute with mild chili paste
    - 1 tablespoon ground cumin
    - 1 tablespoon paprika
    - 1 teaspoon dried oregano
    - 1 teaspoon black pepper
    - 1 teaspoon salt
- **For the Skewers:**
    - 1 lb (450 g) beef heart, cleaned, trimmed, and cut into 1-inch (2.5 cm) cubes
    - Wooden or metal skewers (if using wooden skewers, soak them in water for at least 30 minutes before using)
- **For Serving:**
    - Boiled or roasted potatoes
    - Peruvian corn (or regular corn on the cob)
    - Aji sauce or hot sauce
    - Fresh parsley or cilantro, chopped (for garnish)

Instructions:

1. **Prepare the Marinade:**
    - In a bowl, combine the red wine vinegar, soy sauce, vegetable oil, minced garlic, aji panca paste, aji amarillo paste, ground cumin, paprika, dried oregano, black pepper, and salt. Mix well to combine.
2. **Marinate the Beef Heart:**
    - Place the beef heart cubes in a large resealable plastic bag or bowl. Pour the marinade over the beef heart, making sure all the pieces are well coated.
    - Seal the bag or cover the bowl and refrigerate for at least 4 hours, or overnight for best results.
3. **Prepare the Skewers:**
    - Preheat your grill to medium-high heat.
    - Thread the marinated beef heart cubes onto the skewers, leaving a little space between each piece.
4. **Grill the Anticuchos:**
    - Lightly oil the grill grates to prevent sticking.

- Place the skewers on the grill and cook for about 3-4 minutes per side, or until the beef heart is cooked through and has a nice char. The internal temperature should reach 145°F (63°C).
5. **Serve:**
    - Remove the skewers from the grill and let them rest for a few minutes.
    - Serve the anticuchos hot with boiled or roasted potatoes, Peruvian corn, and a side of aji sauce or hot sauce.
    - Garnish with fresh parsley or cilantro if desired.

Tips:

- **Beef Heart:** If beef heart is not available, you can substitute with other cuts of beef such as sirloin or tenderloin, but the texture and flavor will be different.
- **Marinating Time:** For more intense flavor, marinate the beef heart overnight.

Storage:

- **Refrigeration:** Leftover anticuchos can be stored in an airtight container in the refrigerator for up to 3 days.
- **Freezing:** The marinated beef heart can be frozen before cooking for up to 2 months. Thaw in the refrigerator overnight and proceed with grilling.

Enjoy your **Peruvian Anticuchos**, a delicious and authentic taste of Peru that's perfect for grilling season or any time you crave flavorful skewers!

Colombian Arepas de Queso

Ingredients:

- 2 cups arepa flour (masarepa or harina de maíz, such as P.A.N. brand)
- 1 1/2 cups warm water
- 1 cup shredded cheese (such as mozzarella, or a mix of mozzarella and queso blanco)
- 1/2 teaspoon salt
- 2 tablespoons butter or oil (for cooking)

Instructions:

1. **Prepare the Dough:**
   - In a large mixing bowl, combine the arepa flour and salt.
   - Gradually add the warm water, mixing with your hands or a spoon until a soft dough forms. The dough should be moist but not sticky.
   - Gently fold in the shredded cheese until evenly distributed throughout the dough.
2. **Shape the Arepas:**
   - Divide the dough into 8-10 equal portions. Roll each portion into a ball and then flatten it into a disk about 1/2 inch (1.3 cm) thick. You can use your hands or a flat surface to flatten them.
   - If the dough is too sticky, lightly dust your hands or the surface with a bit of flour.
3. **Cook the Arepas:**
   - Heat a skillet or griddle over medium heat and add a little butter or oil.
   - Place the arepas in the hot skillet and cook for about 5-7 minutes on each side, or until they develop a golden-brown crust and are cooked through. You may need to adjust the heat to ensure they cook evenly without burning.
4. **Serve:**
   - Serve the arepas warm. They can be enjoyed on their own or with a variety of toppings, such as avocado, sour cream, or salsa.

Tips:

- **Cheese:** Use a cheese that melts well for the best results. If using a very salty cheese, you might want to reduce the added salt in the dough.
- **Cooking:** If you prefer a crispier texture, you can cook the arepas in a little more oil. Alternatively, you can bake them in a preheated oven at 375°F (190°C) for 15-20 minutes for a softer crust.

Storage:

- **Refrigeration:** Leftover arepas can be stored in an airtight container in the refrigerator for up to 3 days.
- **Freezing:** Arepas can be frozen for up to 2 months. To reheat, thaw in the refrigerator and then warm in a skillet or oven.

Enjoy your **Colombian Arepas de Queso**, a tasty and versatile treat that's perfect for any time of the day!

Uruguayan Tarta de Espinaca

Ingredients:

- **For the Pastry:**
    - 1 1/2 cups all-purpose flour
    - 1/2 cup unsalted butter, cold and cubed
    - 1/4 cup cold water
    - 1/4 teaspoon salt
- **For the Filling:**
    - 1 tablespoon olive oil
    - 1 large onion, finely chopped
    - 2 cloves garlic, minced
    - 4 cups fresh spinach, washed and chopped (or 1 package frozen spinach, thawed and drained)
    - 1 cup ricotta cheese
    - 1 cup shredded mozzarella cheese
    - 2 large eggs
    - 1/2 cup heavy cream
    - 1/4 teaspoon ground nutmeg
    - Salt and black pepper to taste

Instructions:

1. **Prepare the Pastry:**
    - In a large mixing bowl, combine the flour and salt. Add the cold, cubed butter and use a pastry cutter or your fingers to cut the butter into the flour until the mixture resembles coarse crumbs.
    - Gradually add the cold water, mixing until the dough just comes together. Do not overwork the dough.
    - Form the dough into a disk, wrap it in plastic wrap, and refrigerate for at least 30 minutes.
2. **Prepare the Filling:**
    - Heat olive oil in a large skillet over medium heat. Add the chopped onion and cook until translucent, about 5 minutes. Add the minced garlic and cook for another 1-2 minutes.
    - Add the spinach to the skillet and cook until wilted and any excess moisture has evaporated. If using frozen spinach, make sure it's well-drained.
    - Remove from heat and let the spinach mixture cool slightly.
3. **Prepare the Tart Shell:**
    - Preheat your oven to 375°F (190°C).
    - On a lightly floured surface, roll out the chilled dough to fit a 9-inch (23 cm) tart pan. Gently transfer the dough to the pan, pressing it into the bottom and sides. Trim any excess dough.

- Prick the bottom of the dough with a fork to prevent it from puffing up during baking.

4. **Assemble the Tart:**
    - In a mixing bowl, combine the ricotta cheese, shredded mozzarella, eggs, heavy cream, ground nutmeg, salt, and black pepper. Mix well.
    - Stir in the cooked spinach and onion mixture until evenly combined.
    - Pour the filling into the prepared tart shell and smooth the top.

5. **Bake the Tart:**
    - Bake in the preheated oven for 35-40 minutes, or until the filling is set and the top is golden brown.
    - Allow the tart to cool for a few minutes before slicing and serving.

Tips:

- **Dough:** If you prefer a quicker option, you can use store-bought pie or tart dough.
- **Spinach:** Make sure to squeeze out as much moisture as possible from frozen spinach to prevent a soggy tart.

Storage:

- **Refrigeration:** Leftover tart can be stored in an airtight container in the refrigerator for up to 3 days.
- **Freezing:** The tart can be frozen for up to 2 months. Thaw in the refrigerator overnight before reheating in the oven.

Enjoy your **Uruguayan Tarta de Espinaca**, a flavorful and satisfying dish that's perfect for any occasion!

Venezuelan Hallacas

Ingredients:

- **For the Dough (Masa):**
    - 4 cups cornmeal (harina de maíz)
    - 2 cups chicken or beef broth (warm)
    - 1 cup vegetable oil or lard
    - 1 teaspoon annatto powder (for color, optional)
    - Salt to taste
- **For the Filling:**
    - 1 lb (450 g) beef (such as chuck or brisket), cut into chunks
    - 1 lb (450 g) pork (such as shoulder or belly), cut into chunks
    - 1/2 lb (225 g) ham, chopped
    - 1 large onion, chopped
    - 2 cloves garlic, minced
    - 1 bell pepper, chopped
    - 1/2 cup tomato paste
    - 1/2 cup dry white wine
    - 1 tablespoon ground cumin
    - 1 tablespoon paprika
    - 1 teaspoon ground black pepper
    - 1 teaspoon dried oregano
    - 1/2 teaspoon ground cloves
    - 1/2 teaspoon ground cinnamon
    - 1/2 cup olives, pitted and sliced
    - 1/4 cup capers
    - 1/2 cup raisins
    - 1/2 cup almonds, chopped (optional)
    - Salt to taste
- **For Assembly:**
    - Banana leaves, cut into squares (about 10x10 inches), or parchment paper as an alternative
    - String or kitchen twine

Instructions:

1. **Prepare the Filling:**
    - In a large pot, combine the beef and pork chunks. Cover with water and cook until tender, about 1-1.5 hours. Drain and let cool. Shred the meat or cut it into small pieces.
    - In a large skillet or another pot, heat a bit of oil over medium heat. Sauté the onions, garlic, and bell pepper until soft.
    - Add the tomato paste, white wine, cumin, paprika, black pepper, oregano, cloves, and cinnamon. Cook for a few minutes to blend the flavors.

- Add the shredded meat, ham, olives, capers, raisins, and almonds. Mix well and cook for another 10-15 minutes until the filling is well combined and heated through. Season with salt to taste. Allow the filling to cool.

2. **Prepare the Dough:**
   - In a large bowl, combine the cornmeal, annatto powder (if using), and salt. Gradually add the warm broth, mixing until the dough is smooth and pliable.
   - Add the vegetable oil or lard to the dough and mix until fully incorporated.

3. **Assemble the Hallacas:**
   - Preheat a large pot of water for steaming.
   - If using banana leaves, heat them briefly over an open flame or in a hot skillet to make them more pliable.
   - Lay out a banana leaf square (or parchment paper) on a clean surface. Spread a small amount of dough (about 1/4 inch thick) in the center of the leaf.
   - Add a spoonful of the filling on top of the dough. Fold the sides of the leaf over the filling and then fold the ends to enclose the hallaca.
   - Tie the hallaca with kitchen twine to secure it. Repeat with the remaining dough and filling.

4. **Cook the Hallacas:**
   - Place the wrapped hallacas in the preheated pot of boiling water. Steam for about 1-1.5 hours, or until the dough is cooked through and firm.
   - Alternatively, you can boil the hallacas in a large pot of water for the same amount of time.

5. **Serve:**
   - Let the hallacas cool slightly before unwrapping. Serve warm, either as a main dish or as part of a festive spread.

Tips:

- **Banana Leaves:** If you can't find banana leaves, you can use parchment paper as a substitute, though it won't impart the same flavor.
- **Preparation:** Hallacas are often prepared in large batches due to the time-consuming nature of the process. They can be frozen and reheated, making them ideal for holiday celebrations.

Storage:

- **Refrigeration:** Leftover hallacas can be stored in an airtight container in the refrigerator for up to 1 week.
- **Freezing:** Hallacas can be frozen for up to 3 months. Thaw in the refrigerator before reheating. Reheat by steaming or boiling.

Enjoy making and sharing **Venezuelan Hallacas**, a traditional and cherished dish that brings a taste of Venezuela to your table!

Ecuadorian Encebollado

Ingredients:

- **For the Stew:**
    - 1 lb (450 g) fresh tuna (or substitute with other firm white fish)
    - 2 tablespoons vegetable oil
    - 1 large onion, finely chopped
    - 2 cloves garlic, minced
    - 1 bell pepper, chopped
    - 2 tomatoes, chopped
    - 2 teaspoons ground cumin
    - 1 teaspoon paprika
    - 1/2 teaspoon ground black pepper
    - 1/2 teaspoon dried oregano
    - 1/2 teaspoon achiote powder (optional, for color)
    - 4 cups fish stock or water
    - 1 cup yuca (cassava), peeled and cut into chunks
    - 1-2 tablespoons tomato paste
    - Salt to taste
- **For the Onion Relish:**
    - 1 large onion, thinly sliced
    - 1 tablespoon vinegar (white or red)
    - 1 tablespoon lime juice
    - 1/2 teaspoon salt
    - 1/2 teaspoon sugar
    - 1-2 tablespoons chopped cilantro (optional)
- **For Serving:**
    - Lime wedges
    - Avocado slices
    - Fried plantains or crispy corn (optional)

Instructions:

1. **Prepare the Onion Relish:**
    - In a small bowl, combine the thinly sliced onion with vinegar, lime juice, salt, and sugar. Mix well and let it sit for at least 15 minutes to marinate. Add chopped cilantro if desired.
2. **Prepare the Stew:**
    - Cut the fresh tuna into bite-sized pieces and set aside.
    - In a large pot, heat the vegetable oil over medium heat. Add the chopped onion, garlic, and bell pepper. Sauté until the onion is translucent, about 5 minutes.
    - Add the chopped tomatoes, cumin, paprika, black pepper, oregano, and achiote powder (if using). Cook for another 5 minutes to blend the flavors.
    - Stir in the fish stock or water and bring to a boil.

- Add the yuca chunks and cook until they are tender, about 15-20 minutes.
- Stir in the tomato paste and then add the tuna pieces. Cook for an additional 5-10 minutes, or until the tuna is cooked through and flakes easily with a fork. Season with salt to taste.

3. **Serve:**
    - Ladle the stew into bowls and top with the prepared onion relish.
    - Serve with lime wedges, avocado slices, and a side of fried plantains or crispy corn if desired.

Tips:

- **Yuca:** Make sure to cook the yuca until tender, as it can be quite tough if undercooked. If you can't find yuca, you can substitute with potatoes.
- **Fish:** Fresh tuna is ideal for this recipe, but other firm white fish like snapper or cod can be used as well.

Storage:

- **Refrigeration:** Leftover Encebollado can be stored in an airtight container in the refrigerator for up to 3 days.
- **Freezing:** The stew can be frozen for up to 2 months. Thaw in the refrigerator overnight and reheat thoroughly before serving.

Enjoy making and savoring **Ecuadorian Encebollado**, a comforting and flavorful stew that captures the essence of Ecuadorian cuisine!

Bolivian Fricassé

Ingredients:

- **For the Stew:**
    - 1.5 lbs (700 g) pork (or beef), cut into chunks
    - 2 tablespoons vegetable oil
    - 1 large onion, finely chopped
    - 2 cloves garlic, minced
    - 2 medium tomatoes, chopped
    - 1 bell pepper, chopped
    - 1 tablespoon ground cumin
    - 1 tablespoon paprika
    - 1 teaspoon ground black pepper
    - 1 teaspoon dried oregano
    - 1 teaspoon achiote powder (for color, optional)
    - 2 tablespoons tomato paste
    - 4 cups beef or chicken broth
    - 2 large potatoes, peeled and cut into chunks
    - 1/2 cup frozen peas (optional)
    - Salt to taste
- **For the Sauce:**
    - 1/2 cup heavy cream or evaporated milk
    - 1 tablespoon flour (optional, for thickening)
    - 2 tablespoons chopped fresh cilantro or parsley (for garnish)
- **For Serving:**
    - Cooked rice
    - Sliced avocado (optional)
    - Pickled red onions (optional)

Instructions:

1. **Prepare the Stew:**
    - In a large pot or Dutch oven, heat the vegetable oil over medium heat. Add the pork (or beef) chunks and brown them on all sides.
    - Add the chopped onion and minced garlic to the pot. Cook until the onion is translucent and fragrant, about 5 minutes.
    - Stir in the chopped tomatoes, bell pepper, cumin, paprika, black pepper, oregano, and achiote powder (if using). Cook for another 5 minutes to blend the flavors.
    - Add the tomato paste and mix well.
    - Pour in the broth and bring the mixture to a boil. Reduce heat to low, cover, and simmer for about 1 hour, or until the meat is tender.
    - Add the potatoes and cook for an additional 20-30 minutes, or until the potatoes are tender. If using peas, add them during the last 5 minutes of cooking. Season with salt to taste.

2. **Prepare the Sauce:**
   - In a small bowl, whisk together the heavy cream or evaporated milk with the flour (if using) until smooth. Stir this mixture into the stew and cook for a few more minutes until the sauce thickens slightly.
3. **Serve:**
   - Serve the Fricassé over a bed of cooked rice.
   - Garnish with chopped fresh cilantro or parsley.
   - Add sliced avocado and pickled red onions on the side, if desired.

Tips:

- **Thickening:** If you prefer a thicker sauce, you can increase the amount of flour or use a cornstarch slurry (cornstarch mixed with water) to thicken the stew.
- **Meat:** You can use beef or pork, or a combination of both, depending on your preference.

Storage:

- **Refrigeration:** Leftover Fricassé can be stored in an airtight container in the refrigerator for up to 3 days.
- **Freezing:** The stew can be frozen for up to 2 months. Thaw in the refrigerator overnight before reheating. Reheat thoroughly before serving.

Enjoy making and savoring **Bolivian Fricassé**, a flavorful and satisfying dish that captures the essence of Bolivian cuisine!

Paraguayan Pira Caldo

Ingredients:

- **For the Stew:**
    - 1.5 lbs (700 g) freshwater fish (such as tilapia, catfish, or another firm white fish), cut into pieces
    - 2 tablespoons vegetable oil
    - 1 large onion, chopped
    - 2 cloves garlic, minced
    - 2 bell peppers, chopped (one red, one green)
    - 2 tomatoes, chopped
    - 2 medium carrots, sliced
    - 1 cup yuca (cassava), peeled and cut into chunks
    - 4 cups fish stock or water
    - 1 tablespoon ground cumin
    - 1 teaspoon paprika
    - 1/2 teaspoon dried oregano
    - 1/2 teaspoon ground black pepper
    - 1-2 bay leaves
    - 1 tablespoon tomato paste
    - Salt to taste
    - 1/2 cup chopped fresh cilantro or parsley (for garnish)
- **For the Optional Side:**
    - Cooked rice or mashed potatoes

Instructions:

1. **Prepare the Stew:**
    - Heat the vegetable oil in a large pot over medium heat. Add the chopped onion and garlic, and cook until the onion is translucent and fragrant, about 5 minutes.
    - Add the chopped bell peppers and tomatoes. Cook for another 5 minutes, until the vegetables start to soften.
    - Stir in the tomato paste, cumin, paprika, oregano, black pepper, and bay leaves. Cook for another 2 minutes to blend the flavors.
    - Pour in the fish stock or water and bring to a boil.
    - Add the carrots and yuca to the pot. Reduce heat to low, cover, and simmer for about 20 minutes, or until the yuca and carrots are tender.
    - Add the fish pieces to the pot and cook for another 10-15 minutes, or until the fish is cooked through and flakes easily with a fork.
    - Season with salt to taste and remove the bay leaves.
2. **Garnish and Serve:**
    - Stir in the chopped fresh cilantro or parsley just before serving.
    - Serve the Pira Caldo hot, with a side of cooked rice or mashed potatoes if desired.

Tips:

- **Fish:** Use fresh, firm white fish for the best results. If using frozen fish, ensure it is thoroughly thawed before cooking.
- **Yuca:** If yuca is not available, you can substitute with potatoes or other root vegetables.

Storage:

- **Refrigeration:** Leftover Pira Caldo can be stored in an airtight container in the refrigerator for up to 3 days.
- **Freezing:** The stew can be frozen for up to 2 months. Thaw in the refrigerator overnight before reheating. Reheat thoroughly before serving.

Enjoy making and savoring **Paraguayan Pira Caldo**, a flavorful and nourishing dish that captures the essence of Paraguayan cuisine!

www.ingramcontent.com/pod-product-compliance
Lightning Source LLC
LaVergne TN
LVHW081557060526
838201LV00054B/1934